RIVERBANKS
ZOO AND GARDEN

FORTY WILD YEARS

Palmer "Satch" Krantz and Monique Blanchette Jacobs

Foreword by Jim Maddy

The University of South Carolina Press

Published with the Assistance of the Riverbanks Society

© 2013 University of South Carolina

Published by the University of South Carolina Press
Columbia, South Carolina 29208

www.sc.edu/uscpress

Manufactured in China

22 21 20 19 18 17 16 15 14 13   10 9 8 7 6 5 4 3 2 1

Library of Congress Cataloging-in-Publication Data

Krantz, Satch.
  Riverbanks Zoo and Garden : forty wild years / Satch Krantz and Monique Jacobs.
       pages cm
   Includes index.
    ISBN 978-1-61117-310-9 (hardbound : alk. paper)—ISBN 978-1-61117-311-6 (pbk. : alk. paper)
    ISBN 978-1-61117-312-3 (ebook) 1. Riverbanks Zoo and Garden (Columbia, S.C.) 2. Zoos—
South Carolina—Columbia. I. Jacobs, Monique. II. Title.

QL76.5.U62C65 2013
590.73757—dc23   2013013551

Front matter photographs:
page ii: Two siamangs playfully interact with each other; photograph by Richard W. Rokes;
page vi: grizzly bears frolicking; photograph by Ron Brasington

RIVERBANKS ZOO AND GARDEN

This book is dedicated first and foremost to the citizens and elected officials of Richland and Lexington Counties for faithfully supporting Riverbanks Zoo and Garden for the past forty years. It is also dedicated to those who have served on the Riverbanks Park Commission since 1969 as well as the Riverbanks Society Board of Directors and its thousands of members and volunteers. Finally, and by no means last, this book is dedicated to the many incredibly talented people who have served over the years on staff at Riverbanks. Without them none of this would have been possible.

CONTENTS

CONTENTS

FOREWORD

I always tell people, "If you haven't been to the zoo in thirty years, you've missed some big changes." Modern, accredited zoological institutions have transformed themselves into centers of conservation science; they have become sophisticated educators; they are drivers of tourism and the economy; and they are not only home to unique animal species, but also to some of the most talented, passionate professional people who make it all possible. Riverbanks Zoo and Garden is the embodiment of these qualities, putting Columbia, South Carolina, on the world map of outstanding zoos.

Founded in 1974, Riverbanks Zoo and Garden has thrived under one chief visionary leader for most of its forty-year existence. In 1976 Palmer "Satch" Krantz became the director at Riverbanks. He has gone from being one of the youngest people to lead any zoo to being the longest-serving zoo director at any facility. While Satch's story and the story of the zoo are fundamentally different,

they are also intricately connected and have many common elements.

This book details the amazing story of how Riverbanks Zoo and Garden grew— going from small to medium to large. Yes, today Riverbanks welcomes more than one million guests every year, but the zoo is large in a more important sense. As a physical facility, it has been at the forefront of zoo design, immersing visitors in exhibits that entertain and educate. As a center of human knowledge, the Riverbanks Zoo, as a result of the hard work of the board and staff, has had a transformative influence on the entire zoo and aquarium profession.

I first met Director Satch Krantz of the Riverbanks Zoo in 2006, when I became president and CEO of the Association of Zoos and Aquariums (AZA). It's fair to say that no one has taught me more about zoos and aquariums than Satch, and it's also fair to say that no one has a clearer vision of what he or she can achieve in the future.

Satch became chair of the AZA Board of Directors in 2007 for the second time. He was previously elected to this post in 1988. No other person has served in this capacity twice in the history of the AZA. The fact that his peers again called him to lead is a testament to his knowledge and his vision, not just for Riverbanks but for all zoos and aquariums.

Zoos that meet the high accreditation standards of the AZA are in a different class, meeting the highest standards for animal care, conservation, education, safety, and more. Today there are more than two hundred AZA-accredited zoos and aquariums, but in 1979 the Riverbanks Zoo and Garden became just the twenty-sixth zoo to earn this important distinction. As accreditation standards have risen, some zoos struggle to keep up, while others lead the way, challenging others to achieve excellence. Riverbanks Zoo and Garden has been one of the leading standard setters, pushing all zoos and aquariums to be better and more effective.

More than five hundred staff and volunteers at the zoo demonstrate their commitment to high standards of excellence every day. They have been continually recognized by the zoo and aquarium profession with major awards for achievement in the propagation of rare species, from Toco toucans to black howler monkeys, and for outstanding conservation efforts, from Grevy's zebras to tree kangaroos. AZA has organized more than two hundred programs for the Species Survival Plan (SSP) program, and Riverbanks Zoo and Garden plays a key role in seventy of them, committing time and talent so that Nile hippos and giant leaf-tailed geckos and African lions will always be here for future generations. Accolades for groundbreaking teen-education programs and for contributions to regional tourism show just how meaningful the zoo is to people as well as animals.

Congratulations go to everyone at the Riverbanks Zoo and Garden and to the people of Columbia, South Carolina, for forty wild years of achievement and success. I'm grateful for what you've done and for what you have taught us all, and I'm excited to see where you will lead us over the next forty years.

JIM MADDY, PRESIDENT AND CEO,
ASSOCIATION OF ZOOS AND AQUARIUMS

PREFACE

Three years ago Jonathan Haupt, then interim director and now director of the University of South Carolina Press, contacted Monique Jacobs, Riverbanks Zoo and Garden's membership and communications manager, with an idea. Jonathan and his wife, Lorene, have been Riverbanks Society members since they first moved to South Carolina in 2004. They are also zoo buffs, having now visited dozens of zoos around the country. As a publisher Jonathan is also an avid book collector, and over the years has combined his two passions and collected a number of books chronicling the histories of various zoos. The purpose of his call was to ask if we would be interested in producing a coffee-table book as a potential fundraiser for the zoo's upcoming fortieth anniversary. Our immediate response was: Why not? So here we are—three years, thousands of words, and hundreds of photographs later.

A slight word of caution: this book is not meant to be an exact history of Riverbanks Zoo and Garden. Instead it is a mostly chronological collection—and in some cases recollection—of events, milestones, and personalities (both human and animal) that helped shape Columbia's zoo into one of the best in the country.

Some have said that it is impossible to separate my story from that of Riverbanks. To that I say, "Poppycock." (Those who really know me know that I would likely say something far more colorful.) What *is* virtually impossible is to include by name the—literally—thousands of people who have directly contributed to the zoo's success.

In the early 1960s a group of local businessmen came together to discuss building a small zoo for Columbia's children. This led to Zoo's Who, a citywide, door-to-door fund drive involving hundreds of school-aged volunteers. Next came the Greater Columbia Chamber of Commerce and, in particular, two of its committees (both ably chaired by the late Al Rose) that helped advance the zoo concept from dream to reality. The South Carolina General Assembly later created the Riverbanks Park Special Purpose District (as well as the Riverbanks Park Commission, whose first chairman was Don Barton). And, of course, there were many wonderfully supportive people who served on the Richland and Lexington County Legislative Delegation who bravely voted to fund the zoo's initial construction. All of these people were critical to the zoo's creation. There have been many, many more since then.

Following a decade of political intrigue and planning, Riverbanks Zoo (later Riverbanks Zoo *and* Garden) opened to the public on April 25, 1974. By then I had been working at the nascent zoo for sixteen months, having started on January 3, 1973. I was just twenty-two years old and had been out of college for all of three weeks and, perhaps most interestingly, had never been to a zoo. Little did I realize that forty years later I would still be working at Riverbanks and become the longest-tenured zoo director in the United States.

Looking back, one thing is certain. An incredibly talented team of people was needed to build the zoo. Not just the architects and contractors, but the original zoo staff. Like me, most were just out of college

or had recently returned from Vietnam, and our ranks included artists, arborists, landscapers, and budding animal keepers. As opening day approached, this group of dedicated employees, led by director John Mehrtens, worked round the clock for days on end to ready the new zoo for its first guests.

Following several years of growing pains, Riverbanks Zoo began to prosper. This required an entirely new skill set as marketers, educators, and human resource and horticulture professionals came on board. A volunteer program was established and has since grown to more than two hundred active and vital volunteers. The Riverbanks Society was created, and, in addition to a fiercely dedicated board of directors, thousands of people from throughout the Midlands joined its ranks. As Riverbanks Zoo and Garden grew in stature, so did the list of corporate sponsors. We are indeed grateful to the many businesses that have so generously supported our activities and physical growth.

The ever-growing parade of faithful contributors has continued unabated for the past twenty-five or so years. Riverbanks is especially indebted to the past and current members of Lexington and Richland County Councils who have repeatedly demonstrated their support for Riverbanks by supplementing our operating budget and approving our bond issues. Likewise, more than thirty-three thousand households throughout the Midlands of South Carolina and beyond now belong to Riverbanks Society (the society actually has members from forty-five states as well as Puerto Rico and Canada). Membership dues and contributions now account for more than $2 million in annual income. These funds are critical to our success.

Today Riverbanks employs a workforce of nearly two hundred people. It's interesting to note that only about one-quarter of these are directly involved in animal care. The rest are focused on everything from guest services and public safety to horticulture and maintenance. These wonderful folks are tremendously talented and passionately dedicated to the Riverbanks mission. They make Riverbanks Zoo and Garden what it is—the most popular attraction in South Carolina.

Last, and by no means least, there is the Riverbanks Park Commission, the seven-member governing authority of Riverbanks Zoo and Garden—in other words, my bosses. Appointed by Richland and Lexington County Councils and the Columbia City Council, the commission provides

overall guidance and long-range planning for the zoo. How effective are they? The results speak for themselves. If anyone deserves credit for Riverbanks success, it is the many talented individuals who have faithfully served on the commission since 1969.

Regrettably there is no way to list every individual, organization, or group who played a role in Riverbanks' success, so I would be remiss not to include a blanket apology. If we have left out your name (or your family member's or organization's), I am sincerely sorry. But please know that your contribution made a difference, and I thank you for being an integral part of the success of Riverbanks Zoo and Garden.

Finally, regarding this venture, I would like to acknowledge Monique Jacobs. Not only did she act on Jonathan Haupt's initial phone call, but she also coordinated much of the project. This book would not have reached completion without her efforts—and for that I am grateful.

SATCH KRANTZ, PRESIDENT AND CEO,
RIVERBANKS ZOO AND GARDEN

Flamingos in snow. Photograph by Matt Croxton.

ACKNOWLEDGMENTS

Throughout its forty-year history, Riverbanks Zoo and Garden has taken pride in the exceptional teamwork that has helped lead to its success. This book would not have been possible without the collective expertise, details, and images provided by staff, volunteers, and members of the community. We would like to thank the following individuals and organizations for their important contributions, from oral history and profile content to research, facts, and figures: Association of Zoos and Aquariums; Don Barton; Debra Bloom; Paul Brawley; Keith Benson; Kim Benson; Andy Cabe; Elizabeth Clemens; George Davis; John Davis; Ed Diebold; Steve Feldman; Sean Foley; Stacy Hitt; Jerry Howard; Liz Snyder Jumpp; Tim Lewthwaite; Kate Lyngle-Cowand; Dave Nellermoe; Beth Owens; Scott Pfaff; Jennifer Rawlings; Susan Reno; Richland County Auditors Office; Richland County Public Library; Amanda Segura; Melodie Scott-Leach; Bob Seibels; Christine Talleda; Martin Vince; and Christie Vondrak. Thanks also go to Norma Higgins, Susan O'Cain, Marc Rapport, and Alexandra Smith for providing feedback and extra sets of reading eyes when we needed it most. We also thank the many talented eyes behind the camera: Lochlan Baskin; Ron Brasington; Andy Cabe; Larry Cameron; Matt Croxton; Sean Foley; Lynn Hackett; Sue Pfaff; Richard W. Rokes; Lorianne Riggin; and Robin Vondrak; as well as Dixie Allan, Ashley Walker, and all the other staff and volunteers (past and present) who captured remarkable Riverbanks moments that may be included in these pages. A special thank you is owed to Anne-Marie Asbill, who spent countless volunteer hours digitizing thousands of slides in our photo collection; and a heartfelt thanks

ACKNOWLEDGMENTS

goes to the many Riverbanks members who mailed, emailed, and even hand-delivered their favorite pictures and stories of special moments at the zoo and garden. Finally, we want to thank the Riverbanks Park Commission, the Riverbanks Society, and our own families for their amazing support and patience during this project.

INTRODUCTION

An Award-winning Zoo and Garden

By almost any measure, Riverbanks Zoo and Garden is an institution of regional and national significance:

Two-time winner of the Governor's Cup as South Carolina's Most Outstanding Tourist Attraction by the South Carolina Chamber of Commerce;

Voted Outstanding Regional Attraction by the Capital City/Lake Murray Tourism Region;

Three-time winner as "Travel Attraction of the Year" by the Southeast Tourism Society;

Hailed by *Horticulture* magazine as one of the nation's ten gardens that inspire;

Named one of twenty great botanical gardens and arboretums across North America by HGTV;

Voted "Conservation Organization of the Year" by the South Carolina Wildlife Federation and National Wildlife Federation;

Five-time winner of the prestigious Edward H. Bean Award by the Association of Zoos and Aquariums;

Three-time winner of the International Conservation Award by the Association of Zoos and Aquariums.

Recognized today as one of America's best zoos, Riverbanks Zoo and Garden began in the early 60s as the dream of a handful of

Columbia-area business leaders, who envisioned a small children's zoo featuring cows, chickens, raccoons, and other native wildlife. While their dream never materialized, their effort was later incorporated into a grand plan to develop a large park on the banks of the lower Saluda River.

The zoo's first executive director, John Mehrtens, added an intriguing layer to the Riverbanks story. A bombastic native of the Bronx, New York, Mehrtens possessed a "damn the torpedoes" attitude and was determined to build what he considered the perfect zoo. When the Columbia Zoological Park finally opened on April 25, 1974, residents were both confused and proud—confused by the fact that the small children's zoo had somehow grown into a full-blown zoological park with lions, tigers, and bears, yet proud that Columbia now had something that could not be found in Atlanta, Charlotte, or Charleston.

In the first six years after opening, however, the zoo struggled. Its name was changed to Riverbanks Zoo, Mehrtens's firing was front-page news, and vital operating funds were withheld by the local governments. By the summer of 1976, Palmer "Satch" Krantz had been hired as executive director. That decision, combined with a change in philosophy of the zoo's governing board, led to a reassessment of the park and its position in the community.

The tide turned in 1980 as local governments came together to stabilize the zoo's finances. As a result Riverbanks experienced a period of planned and sustained growth throughout the 1980s, and by 1990 Riverbanks was recognized as one of America's best small zoos with an annual attendance of 850,000 visitors.

Energized by this success, Riverbanks crossed the lower Saluda River in 1995 to develop a seventy-acre botanical garden. Designed by one of the nation's premiere

(facing) Two elephants splashing. Photograph by Richard W. Rokes. (below) Amur tiger and cubs.

A crowd eagerly waits for the sea lion demonstration to begin.

garden design firms, Environmental Planning and Design of Pittsburgh, Riverbanks Botanical Garden garnered almost immediate national attention and has since been hailed by *Horticulture* magazine as one of the nation's ten gardens that inspire and by HGTV as one of the twenty great botanical gardens and arboretums across North America.

The turn of the twenty-first century brought Riverbanks' most ambitious expansion. Dubbed Zoo 2002, this $20 million project built a state-of-the-art birdhouse and recreated Africa's Ndoki Forest with elephants, gorillas and meerkats. The project also constructed a mile-long road in West Columbia leading to a new, dedicated entrance at Riverbanks Botanical Garden. During this time South Carolina developed an extraordinary sister-state relationship with Queensland, Australia, resulting in the premier of Queensland gifting Riverbanks with two highly sought-after koalas. These remarkable major exhibits and improvements helped propel Riverbanks into world-class status.

Today Riverbanks Zoo and Garden is one of the best-attended zoos in the United States, welcoming more than one million guests each year. And, in a city with a metropolitan population of about seven hundred thousand, the zoo's private, nonprofit support organization, Riverbanks Society, boasts more than thirty-three thousand member households, making it one of the largest zoo societies per capita in the nation.

While the roles of zoos and botanical gardens continually evolve, unstable economic conditions threaten to weaken funding from both public and private sectors. Nevertheless Riverbanks continues to thrive, fighting the odds with creative initiatives designed to enhance the guest experience, generate public interest, and produce much-needed revenue that will carry on the ultimate mission: to foster an appreciation and concern for all living things.

On April 25, 2014, Riverbanks will celebrate forty years of connecting individuals, families, and groups with the world's wildlife and wild places. The years leading up to this milestone—and the trails that blazed the way for South Carolina's largest gated attraction—are layered with history, personality, and stories that long to be shared with the citizens of the Midlands and beyond. Thanks to the foresight of various supporters and the assistance of Riverbanks Society, we are now able to do just that.

Awards and Achievements Timeline

1974
Most Outstanding Tax-Supported Attraction, South Carolina Chamber of Commerce

1975
Conservation Organization of the Year, South Carolina Wildlife Federation and National Wildlife Federation

1977
Most Outstanding Tax-Supported Attraction, South Carolina Chamber of Commerce

(top) Stunning even at night, the Botanical Garden provides a perfect setting for after-hours events, weddings and receptions. (bottom) Riverbanks is one of only a handful of institutions in the United States that keep gentoo penguins.

Riverbanks shattered its weekly attendance record during spring break of 2010, one of the busiest seasons on record, drawing a total of 68,513 visitors in that single week.

1978
Significant Achievement Award for Captive Propagation of the Toco Toucan, Association of Zoos and Aquariums

1981
Significant Achievement Award for Captive Propagation of the White-faced Saki, Association of Zoos and Aquariums | Significant Achievement Award for Captive

Propagation of the Black Howler Monkey, Association of Zoos and Aquariums | Governor's Cup for South Carolina's Most Outstanding Attraction, South Carolina Chamber of Commerce

1982
Edward H. Bean Award for Most Notable Birth, Black Howler Monkey, Association of Zoos and Aquariums

1983
Significant Achievement Award for Ground Cuscus Breeding Program, Association of Zoos and Aquariums

1985
Most Outstanding Tax-Supported Attraction, South Carolina Chamber of Commerce

1986
Most Outstanding Tax-Supported Attraction, South Carolina Chamber of Commerce

1989
Travel Attraction of the Year, Southeast Tourism Society | Most Outstanding Non-Recurring Event, Opening of the Aquarium-Reptile Complex, South Carolina Chamber of Commerce

1990
Significant Achievement Award in Exhibit Design for the Aquarium-Reptile Complex, Association of Zoos and Aquariums | Attendance breaks one million, sets record (1,019,834)

1993
Travel Attraction of the Year, Southeast Tourism Society

1994
Most Outstanding Non-Recurring Event, 10th Anniversary Celebration, South Carolina Chamber of Commerce

1998
Edward H. Bean Award for Long-term Propagation of Ramphastids [toucans], Association of Zoos and Aquariums

By 2010 Riverbanks had proved itself the largest gated attraction in the South, providing inspiration for a no. 1 attraction campaign. One of a series of four concepts designed by the artists at Chernoff Newman, this image appeared on billboards along interstates between Augusta and Charlotte.

2002

Attendance breaks one million, sets new record (1,020,876) | Governor's Cup Award for South Carolina's Most Outstanding Attraction, South Carolina Chamber of Commerce | Outstanding Regional Attraction Award, Capital City/Lake Murray Country Tourism Region | Travel Attraction of the Year, Southeast Tourism Society | International Conservation Award for Tree Kangaroo Conservation Program, Association of Zoos and Aquariums | Significant Achievements Award in Exhibits for Riverbanks Avian Program, Association of Zoos and Aquariums

2004

Education Award Top Honors for "Teens in Action" program, Association of Zoos and Aquariums

2005

Edward H. Bean Award for Long-term Propagation and Captive Husbandry of the Malagasy Leaf-tailed Gecko, Association of Zoos and Aquariums

2007

John Behler Scholarship—for herpetology keeper to attend the Association of Zoos and Aquariums Crocodilian Management School

2009

Attendance exceeds one million (1,006,170)

2010

Edward H. Bean Significant Achievement Award for Long-term Propagation and Husbandry of the Black-footed Cat, Association of Zoos and Aquariums Attendance exceeds one million (1,015,201)

2011

Columbia Choice Award for Site Beautification Management, Columbia Green and Columbia Tree & Appearance Commission | Edward H. Bean Award for Long-term Propagation and Management of the Bali Mynah, Association of Zoos and Aquariums | Outstanding Achievement Award, Lexington Soil and Water Conservation District | Attendance exceeds one million (1,000,224)

2012

Attendance soars to all-time high (1,029,492) | Named one of America's Top 10 zoos by TripAdvisor (ranked no. 4) | Wildlife Conservation Award, South Carolina Wildlife Federation | Earth Day Award for Riverbanks comPOOst program, South Carolina Department of Health and Environmental Control | International Conservation Award for support of the Grevy's Zebra Trust program, Association of Zoos and Aquariums

(above) Throughout her first year, Yara the Hamadryas baboon could frequently be seen hitching a ride on Mom's back. Photograph by Richard W. Rokes. (overleaf) Koala and joey. Photograph by Richard W. Rokes.

Chapter 1

THE EARLY YEARS

Contrary to popular belief, Riverbanks is neither Columbia's first zoo nor its second. Around the turn of the twentieth century, Columbia actually had two zoos.

In 1897 the fifteen-acre Hyatt Park opened in Eau Claire, the city's first suburban neighborhood. The park, developed by North Carolina–born Frederick H. Hyatt, featured a two-story pavilion, or "casino," with a five-hundred-seat auditorium for vaudeville performances and concerts. It also boasted a café, soda fountain, shooting gallery and bowling alley. In addition the park was home to Columbia's first zoo, housing an array of animals from a black bear, an alligator, rabbits, possums, porcupines, and deer to Japanese pheasants, an unknown species of bird referred to in various accounts as a "Mexican cockatoo,"

ring-tailed and Java monkeys, lemurs, ocelots, and coyotes. Hyatt Park's zoo operated until 1909. The pavilion continued to accommodate a handful of public events until it was demolished after World War I.

Four years later Irwin Park opened to the public on what is today the site of the city's water treatment plant and Riverfront Park. The brain child of waterworks engineer John Irwin, the park is said to have been constructed by plant employees in their spare time. Along with a fountain, ponds, and a bandstand, the park featured a small zoo with swans, geese, ducks, owls, camels, deer, elk, ostriches, monkeys, bears, and goats.

In hopes of demonstrating support for the Irwin Park Zoo, the first zoological society in Columbia was formed. By 1915 the

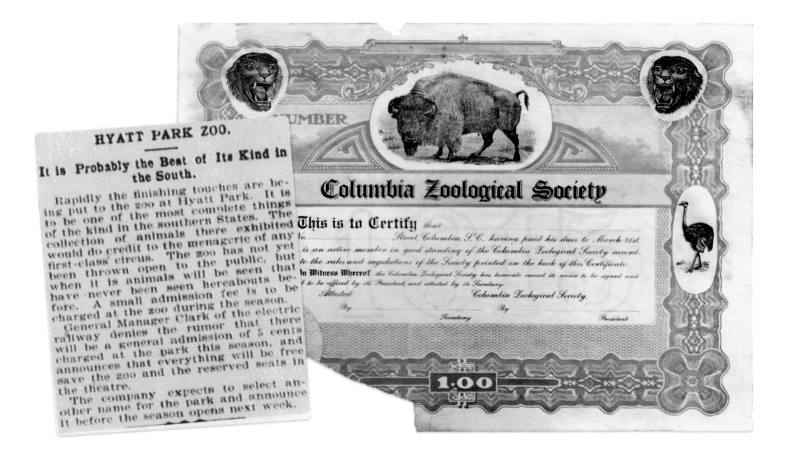

HYATT PARK ZOO.

It is Probably the Best of Its Kind in the South.

Rapidly the finishing touches are being put to the zoo at Hyatt Park. It is to be one of the most complete things of the kind in the southern States. The collection of animals there exhibited would do credit to the menagerie of any first-class circus. The zoo has not yet been thrown open to the public, but when it is animals will be seen that have never been seen hereabouts before. A small admission fee is to be charged at the zoo during the season.

General Manager Clark of the electric railway denies the rumor that there will be a general admission of 5 cents charged at the park this season, and announces that everything will be free save the zoo and the reserved seats in the theatre.

The company expects to select another name for the park and announce it before the season opens next week.

Columbia Zoological Society

This is to Certify that

No. .... *Street, Columbia, S.C. having paid his dues to March 31st,*

is an active member in good standing of the Columbia Zoological Society accord-

to the rules and regulations of the Society printed on the back of this Certificate.

In Witness Whereof the Columbia Zoological Society has hereunto caused its name to be signed and

to be affixed by its President and attested by its Secretary.

Attested   *Columbia Zoological Society.*

By ....   *By* ....

Secretary   *President*

1.00

(left) The State, May 5, 1901, p.8. (right) One of the original member certificates issued by the Columbia Zoological Society c. 1915.

society was offering lithographed membership certificates in exchange for annual dues of one dollar; a lifetime membership went for ten dollars. Animal donations were also accepted by the society. In the spring of that year, a local doctor told the press that he would consider donating a wild boar to the zoo, but only if the sign outside a Lady Amherst Pheasant display was removed

because apparently the exhibit was occupied by a common crow.

In 1916 several anecdotal stories appeared in the *State*. On February 24 one item reported that a new employee of the zoo, who was also an animal trainer with circus experience, intended to "train the animals in many smart things," and he started out by taking on a wild cat with "serious

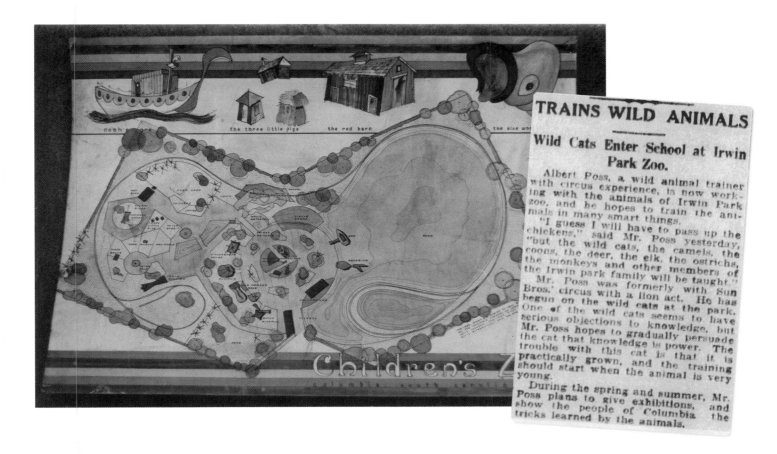

TRAINS WILD ANIMALS

Wild Cats Enter School at Irwin Park Zoo.

Albert Poss, a wild animal trainer with circus experience, is now working with the animals of Irwin Park zoo, and he hopes to train the animals in many smart things.

"I guess I will have to pass up the chickens," said Mr. Poss yesterday, "but the wild cats, the camels, the coons, the deer, the elk, the ostrichs, the monkeys and other members of the Irwin park family will be taught."

Mr. Poss was formerly with Sun Bros.' circus with a lion act. He has begun on the wild cats at the park. One of the wild cats seems to have serious objections to knowledge, but Mr. Poss hopes to gradually persuade the cat that knowledge is power. The trouble with this cat is that it is practically grown, and the training should start when the animal is very young.

During the spring and summer, Mr. Poss plans to give exhibitions, and show the people of Columbia the tricks learned by the animals.

objections to knowledge." Another chronicled on October 12 that a North Carolina fruit farmer selling apples in Columbia had "hinted to the Irwin Park management" that he wanted them to take a four-hundred-pound bear named Mr. Bruin off his hands, "that is, of course, if the management is willing to pour a goodly number of dollars into the apple grower's cart." Another piece

on December 30 recounted how a local businessman caught a six-foot rattlesnake, showed it off to all of his friends and customers, and then ultimately donated it to the zoo as a tribute to his own snake-catching skills.

At the time Irwin Park was a refreshing addition to the community. A reminiscent piece in the *Columbia Record* dated May 9,

(left) The original concept for the Riverbanks Park was a children's zoo featuring a storybook theme with exhibit names such as Noah's Ark and Three Little Pigs. (right) The State, May 15, 1901, p. 9.

Happy the Tiger remains a celebrity at Riverbanks. This bronze sculpture—a favorite family photo op— was donated by Stanley O. Smith, Jr., and his family in honor of the individuals and organizations whose early funding led to the development of Riverbanks.

1946, claimed "it was almost the only public park in Columbia and the meeting place of the majority of the city's children and nurses." Irwin Park ultimately was dismantled during World War I because of the growing water demands by soldiers at Fort Jackson. Almost fifty years would pass before the citizens of Columbia could claim a zoo of their own.

Happy the Tiger

In 1964 Columbia, South Carolina, service-station owner O. Stanley (Stan) Smith bought a baby tiger. Unlike most exotic pet owners, he was not interested in having the most dangerous animal in town. Instead he wanted to promote his popular Gervais Street gas station and carwash. The service station was affiliated with Esso (now part of ExxonMobil), and the big oil company had just launched its famous "Put a Tiger in Your Tank" advertising campaign.

Smith purchased the two-week-old female tiger cub from Chicago's Lincoln Park Zoo, at the time managed by legendary zoo director and TV personality Marlin Perkins. But Smith's intentions were not

Bamboo—*Bambusa multiplex* 'Alphonso-Karrii'

COLOR: Yellow clumps with green striping
BLOOMING PERIOD: Grown for foliage
TYPE: Clumping Bamboo
SIZE: 15 to 20 feet tall
EXPOSURE: Full sun

People often cringe at the word "bamboo." Riverbanks staff receive more calls from people wanting to rid their yard of bamboo than from people who want to plant the right kind. Bamboo does not need to be feared; clumping varieties such as 'Alphonso-Karrii' will not take over your yard (or your neighbor's). This variety is especially nice for the color it adds to the garden with its yellow and green-striped canes.

Alphonso-Karrii boasts striped canes. Photograph by Matt Croxton.

entirely proprietary. He was also active in community affairs, especially with an initiative to develop a zoo for the children of Columbia. Efforts to build the zoo had so far failed, and interest seemed to be waning, so he hoped a live tiger would rekindle the public's attention at a critical juncture. Smith also hoped that, in addition to driving gasoline sales and car washes, the tiger would serve as a living symbol for the future zoo.

The cub was soon housed in a replicated circus wagon parked against an outer wall of the carwash office. People flocked to see her, but there was a problem: the little tiger didn't have a name. Ever the marketer, Smith held a city-wide naming contest, bringing even more publicity to his establishment. Competition was fierce; it seemed like everyone in Columbia wanted to name the community's new four-legged celebrity. On March 8, 1965, a medical technician at Columbia's VA hospital, Hattie Johns, was announced the winner with her submission "Happy the Tiger." As part of the grand prize, Johns would have the honor of donating the tiger to the future zoo in her name.

Happy the Tiger was ultimately moved to the zoo and housed in one of a string of eleven glass-fronted exhibits in Small Mammal North (later renamed Riverbanks Conservation Outpost). She became known throughout South Carolina and, as Smith had hoped, helped provide the motivation needed to jumpstart efforts to develop the zoo-a zoo that would ultimately become one of the most successful in the United States. Happy died in 1979 at the age of fifteen. Smith commissioned a statue in her honor, which today can be seen just across from the original tiger exhibit at Riverbanks.

Columbia Zoological Society

In the early 1960s a prominent group of local business leaders, headed by Albert Heyward, formed the Columbia Zoological Society. Their goal was to develop a small children's zoo just outside of the city-proper on the banks of the Saluda River. While little written documentation survives from their efforts, they were clearly instrumental in providing the spark that would soon ignite the creation of Riverbanks Zoo. Among the society's most notable accomplishments was bringing to Columbia famed zoo director Marlin Perkins for advice on site selection. (It's interesting to note that one of the sites identified was off Garners Ferry Rd. near the VA Hospital). The society also acquired sixteen acres of land along the Saluda River from South Carolina Electric and Gas and a small wood-framed house that would later serve as the zoo's first administration building.

By 1965 an optimistic society had developed plans for a zoo that would cost between $300,000 and $350,000. The group proposed admission fees of 25 cents for adults and 10 cents for children, which based on their projected attendance, would generate about $24,000 in revenue each year. With this in mind, the society set out to raise money to build their zoo and launched a fundraising campaign called Zoo's Who. In conjunction with donations received from the Columbia and Richland County Sertoma Clubs, the society ultimately raised around $60,000, far short of their $300,000 goal. The project fizzled after a few years because of a lack of funding, but the Columbia Zoological Society

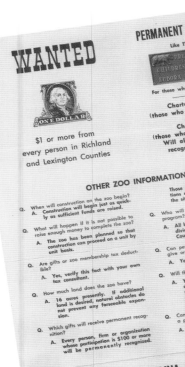

In one of the first major fundraising efforts for the proposed zoo, schoolchildren went door-to-door seeking donations for the park. In exchange for contributions of one dollar, donors were issued a bright yellow "Zoo's Who" tag, which served as an advance ticket to the grand opening of the zoo.

This baby siamang looks almost too cute to hoot and holler. Among the zoo's most iconic animals are the howling monkeys, who are in fact not monkeys at all but siamangs—members of the ape family from Southeast Asia.

Riverfront Recreation

Columbia, South Carolina, sits at the confluence of two rivers—the Broad and Saluda—that on meeting form the Congaree River. In essence Columbia was a planned city, having been selected by the state legislature in 1786 to be the site of South Carolina's new capital because of its centralized location. From the city's inception, the riverfront area was considered undesirable, since it housed warehouses, wharfs, taverns, and more than one house of ill repute, and for much of the twentieth century Columbia's riverfront property remained largely inaccessible and undeveloped, a tangle of abandoned buildings, vines, and thick undergrowth.

But in the mid-1960s a group of area business leaders set out to change this dynamic as they set their sights on developing an extensive park on a beautiful 500-acre tract of land on either side of the Saluda River, less than a mile from downtown. They hoped the park, which they initially envisioned as a historic theme park, would breathe life into Columbia's meager tourism industry by turning their sleepy little city into a must-stop destination for people driving between the Northeast and Florida. This, however, would be no easy task. The next several years would prove to be a political battleground for the

remained an active participant in the development of the zoo through the creation of the Riverbanks Park Commission in 1969. The group disbanded shortly thereafter, but their dream of a zoo for Columbia's children served as the motivation behind all that followed.

future of development of a "Riverbanks Park."

The Greater Columbia Chamber of Commerce acted as the catalyst for the park and in 1966 established the River-front Recreation Committee. Al Rose, at the time the general manager of the Tremont Motor Inn in Cayce, emerged as its leader. The committee was charged with studying the development of areas along the Saluda, Broad, and Congaree Rivers.

Virtually untouched since the Civil War, the proposed site was ripe for development. It boasted large granite boulders, towering trees, Spanish moss, mountain laurel, crystal-clear streams, and the ruins of one of South Carolina's first textile mills—all within the shadow of Columbia's growing skyline. Despite its natural beauty, the site was not without challenges, straddling two counties and two municipalities in an area of the state not known for regional cooperation.

The committee recognized it faced a political nightmare, given the differing governmental bodies with authority over portions of the site, and agreed that a creative form of cooperation would be needed if the project were to succeed, but its first focus would be to develop a comprehensive list of park facilities. A rather extensive and eclectic list was compiled at a November 9,

1966, meeting and included everything from a zoo, outdoor drama area, and botanical gardens to a textile-mill museum, restored covered bridge, and picnic areas.

Approximately six months later the committee issued a report listing all the components that would make up the proposed State Park–Recreation Complex and concluded with this prophetic statement:

The unit considered by this Committee to have top priority in the complex's development is the zoo. There are several reasons for this. First, the zoological society presently has the deed for 16 plus acres for the zoo's development within the area being considered. Second, extensive progress has been made both financially and with the acquisition of animals, to where involvement for completion is minimal. Third, the zoo is compatible with the project and would contribute much to its acceptance.

Please allow us to elaborate further on this subject. Originally intended to be a small children's zoo when the idea originated several years ago, it gained public interest and support as it matured to where it has now reached the stage where plans call for a complete zoo with facilities and attractions to serve the

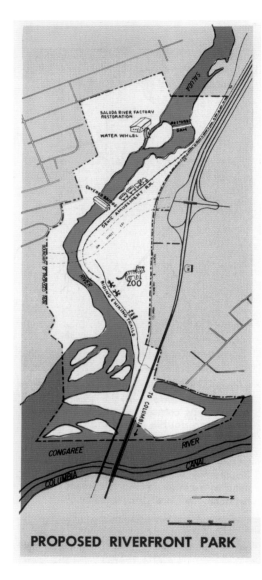

PROPOSED RIVERFRONT PARK

One of the earliest known illustrations of the proposed riverfront park. This map shows the intended locations of the zoo, a restored Saluda River Factory, a covered bridge, and a miniature railroad along the river. Source: 1967 City of Columbia annual report.

entire state. The zoo site has already seen many of the first stage improvements implemented such as complete chain-link fencing, clearing of underbrush, access roads and more recently the acquisition of a large frame house suitable for offices and living quarters for a caretaker.

Local business firms have pledged numerous materials and facilities to the actual construction of the zoo. Bricks have been contributed for the retaining wall and the costs of many of the individual units have been pledged for those specific purposes. One such pledge is for a "contact corral" where school children, with proper supervision, can actually touch and feel certain animals to be included in the zoo. Animals should prove to be no problem as many have already been pledged by reliable persons and businesses and many more are available from other zoos.

The society strongly believes that the great amount of interest as expressed by thousands of local and state citizens through their monetary and other contributions and the vast number of inquiries that have been made concerning the zoo's progress, is impressive evidence that the people of this area want a zoo and would support it.

Further evidence of a regional buy-in appeared in an article from the September 8, 1967, edition of the *State* newspaper, titled "$1.2 Million Park Is Being Planned." The piece stated that a "massive" tourist park might soon be built and that the Richland and Lexington County Legislative Delegations would seek state and federal funds to do so. Some of the projects identified for the proposed park included a zoo, a children's train, and a "replica of a Southern town." An unnamed member of the Lexington delegation was cited as saying, "It's something we need desperately," suggesting strong regional support for the park.

Tricentennial Commission

In 1966 South Carolina approached the three hundredth anniversary of the 1670 landing of English settlers near present-day Charleston. In anticipation of the event, the South Carolina General Assembly created the Tricentennial Commission to plan and implement a statewide celebration. While celebratory events were being planned throughout the state, the three metropolitan areas—Charleston, Columbia and Greenville—were specifically charged with developing a permanent exhibit to commemorate each of the three centuries.

The City of Columbia and Richland County were to commemorate the state's

Delegation OK's Park Along River

The Richland County Legislature Delegation has joined its Lexington County counterpart in approving a River Banks Park planned for both banks of the Saluda River.

The delegation's approval came only after a paragraph was added to the resolution expressing the delegation's "hope" that the land for the park can be acquired without condemnation.

Of the approximately 600 acres involved, about one third is in the river bottom.

All but about seven acres of the land on the Richland County side is owned by the S. C. Electric and Gas Co. There are plans for the building of a high rise apartment building on the seven acres owned by other private property owners.

The delegation, meeting in its regular session Thursday, also proposed a joint 15-member committee to supervise low-cost housing in Richland County.

Members of the committee would be appointed by the city, the County Board of Administrators and the county delegation.

"The committee would investigate, recommend and keep up on national proposals. It would promote the development of private and public low-cost housing as a means of fighting slums," Sen. Hyman Rubin said.

He said he had consulted with members of both City Council and the Board of Administrators before offering the proposal to the delegation.

There are three groups involved in low-rent housing development in the area. The Columbia Housing Authority has supervision in the city. Regional Housing Authority has supervision outside the city limits and a private group has recently been organized to seek federal funds for this purpose.

The issue has been complicated by a ruling of the State Development Board that the Columbia Housing Authority can extend its jurisdiction outside the city limits.

In other matters, the delegation referred to a subcommittee a letter from J. P. Rast asking the delegation to help obtain the opening of College Street across the Southern Railway tracks between Green and Harden streets.

Sen. Walter J. Bristow Jr. said it was his understanding there was a right-of-way across the tracks, but the railroad must provide signaling equipment before it will become usable.

Rast, chairman of the traffic committee for the Five Points Merchants Association, said the street would help relieve congestion.

The State, *October 7, 1967.*

middle century, but from the outset community leaders struggled to identify a project appropriate to that period. The continued debate over a Columbia site soon attracted the attention of the Chamber of Commerce's Riverfront Recreation Committee, and it quickly focused on convincing the Tricentennial Commission to incorporate some or all of Riverbanks Park into Columbia's permanent exhibit.

Since the projects would be financed largely by the state legislature, the committee concentrated their initial efforts on convincing both Richland and Lexington County Legislative Delegations that their park project was worthy of consideration. They appeared to be successful. On October 7, 1967, news of the decision by Richland and Lexington Counties to approve the Riverbanks Park project appeared in the local papers.

With the support of the two counties in hand, the chamber's subcommittee was free to turn its full attention on convincing the Tricentennial Commission that the proposed park was a fitting historical tribute. Al Rose and other park supporters appeared before the Richland County Legislative Delegation and Jim Barnett, director of the South Carolina Tricentennial Commission, on November 28, 1967. Rose asked that the Tricentennial Commission assume

ownership of the Riverbanks Park study. The request generated considerable discussion, but a final decision was delayed because no one knew for certain what would become of the three permanent exhibits once the Tricentennial Celebration ended. Depending on the fate of the exhibits, the two legislative delegations were asked to decide whether the future park should be state or county operated.

Approximately one month later, the Chamber of Commerce's Riverfront Recreation Committee released the results of its work, recommending that the Tricentennial Commission develop a state park along the Saluda River. A budget of $1,160,500 was proposed to fund the construction of the Columbia Zoo and its nearby historical attractions.

With the chamber's work presumably now over, park supporters continued focusing their attention on the permanent location for the tricentennial project. They conducted an all-out assault on the Tricentennial Commission, beginning with a letter-writing campaign extolling the virtues of the Riverbanks site. South Carolina Electric and Gas president Arthur Williams was contacted about making a firm commitment on the land needed for the park, in hopes that he would make the Tricentennial Commission an offer they could not refuse—free land.

On May 2, 1968, Al Rose appeared before a joint meeting of the Columbia-area Tricentennial Commission, Columbia City Council, the Richland County Board of Administrators, and the Richland County Legislative Delegation to request that they consider locating the exhibit on the River-banks site. While Rose presented a spirited and passionate argument, Mrs. James F. Dreher, representing the Historic Columbia Foundation, offered the assembled officials an alternative site—downtown Columbia. The foundation had long been interested in obtaining the old Hampton-Preston Man-sion and combining it with the nearby his-toric Robert Mills House, thereby creating a historic home corridor within the city limits.

The exact location of the Tricentennial's exhibit site was finally determined less than a week later when the City of Columbia and the Richland County Board of Administra-tors agreed to contribute $150,000 each towards the purchase of the entire 1600 block of Laurel Street (the site of the Hamp-ton-Preston Mansion). Later that same day, the South Carolina House Ways and Means Committee voted unanimously to give first reading approval to amend their omnibus bond bill by adding $900,000 to the tri-centennial project.

The decision to locate the exhibit in downtown Columbia appeared to be a

Frogmouth chick.

dagger in the heart of park supporters. Instead the decision proved to be Riverbanks' salvation because had the commission cho-sen the park site for its tricentennial project, it is likely that Riverbanks Zoo would never have been built at all.

Lexington County representatives Ryan Shealy and Jarvis Klapman were outraged at the Tricentennial Commission's decision and vowed to amend the state bond bill in its third and final reading by substituting the Riverbanks Park site for the downtown

Bamboo Muhly—*Muhlenbergia dumosa*

COLOR: Green foliage
BLOOMING PERIOD:
Grown for foliage
TYPE: Ornamental grass
SIZE: 4 feet tall
EXPOSURE: Full sun

Grasses, grasses every-where. Trying to emulate the African plains means that Riverbanks is packed with ornamental grasses. Bamboo muhly is one of

Photograph by Matt Croxton.

the favorites at Riverbanks because of its great wispy texture. It also comes in handy for filler in flower arrangements. The weeping, bright green leaves mature to a delicate straw color and add winter interest in the garden.

location. Columbia's mayor, Lester Bates, was a strong supporter of the Riverbanks project and assumed the role of mediator, suggesting that somehow both sites could be developed. In May 1968 Columbia City Council announced that it would help to move the Riverbanks project forward, although not at the expense of the Tri-centennial celebration.

On Friday, June 14, 1968, the last day of the legislative session, members of the Lexington County Delegation attempted unsuccessfully to secure state funds for the Riverbanks project. Representative Ryan Shealy stood before his House colleagues and railed against the Hampton-Preston site, calling the plan a fraud. Senator Floyd Spence went so far as to propose allowing

By EDWARD B. BORDEN
Staff Writer

The 120-acre Riverbanks Park project may yet be developed for South Carolina's 1970 Tricentennial celebration.

Though local officials last week approved the 150-year-old Hampton-Preston house as Richland's official project, Columbia City Council said Wednesday it would "provide the initiative to make the Riverbanks project a reality" for the state's 300th birthday.

And Lexington County Rep. Ryan C. Shealy said he would seek to have the park project subsituted for the Hampton-Preston house in the omnibus bond bill now on the House floor. The bill passed second reading Wednesday and is up for third and final reading this morning.

Acquisition of land and development of the Hampton-Preston house will cost $1.2 million, of which $900,000 will be derived from state general obligation bonds. Richland County and the city of Columbia have pledged $150,000 each toward the project.

COST ESTIMATE

Site development of the Riverbanks project has been estimated at $250,000. Funds would have to come from local sources or from other federal-state aid.

The Hampton-Preston house, located in the 1600 block of Laurel Street and directly across from the restored Robert Mills house, was Richland's first choice as a historical project for the Tricentennial celebration. The Riverbanks Park was second.

"We're in the process of sub-

mitting a positive program for the area," Columbia Mayor Lester L. Bates said. He did not elaborate on what steps the city would take to begin development of the Park.

TWO MILES FROM CITY

The park, located two miles above Columbia on both banks of the Saluda River near its intersection with the Broad, would necessarily involve governments of both Richland and Lexington counties. Sixty acres lie in each county.

"The natural setting and the historical involvement of the area would prove to be much more attractive to tourists than the (Hampton-Preston) house," Shealy said. "I also feel it would be cheaper, more practical and more diversified."

Shealy said he "could not in good conscience" support a move to develop the Riverbanks

system through financial means other than by Tricentennial funds.

"I could not support it too enthusiastically when I know that millions of dollars are being spent in a place that would not have the attraction of this one," he said.

KLAPMAN 'NOT PLEASED'

Lexington Rep. Jarvis Klapman said he was "not too pleased with the dropping of the Riverbanks project. I'm a little bit disappointed about not being informed (by Richland County officials) on this situation. I didn't know their choice until we read it in the newspapers."

Columbia City Councilmen voted unanimously to support the Hampton-Preston house, but at least three — Mayor Bates and councilmen William Ouzts

and John Campbell — also leaned heavily for the Riverbanks park. Campbell was absent when the vote was taken last May 2.

"There's no reason why we can't support two projects," said Bates. "We can rent the land for 25 years for a nominal fee. We should be able to finance the development through some means. We can't wait forever to get started on this (Riverbanks) project."

Bates said the part proposed by the city for development would encompass that suggested as the Tricentennial park. It would include two foot bridges (one covered), and a paved access road. Attractions would include the old Saluda Factory mill, 130-year-old stone dam, a possible chairlift, part of the Old Cherokee Trail, and the rapids.

The site would also be adjacent to the property for the proposed Columbia Zoo.

Senators from the Richland and Lexington legislative delegations Wednesday said they would support development of the Riverbanks project — but the only problem would be finances.

"It's a fine idea," said Richland Sen. Walter J. Bristow Jr. "I've been interested in this project for quite a while. Funds can be made available ultimately, but I don't know at this time."

Lexington Sen. Floyd Spence said he "is" in agreement with development of the Riverbanks project. But I don't know where the money will come from. We certainly don't have any excess funds in Lexington County."

"Riverbanks Park Still in the Running," The State, May 9, 1968.

Black howler monkeys have been a part of the Riverbanks collection since 1974.

Riverbanks project. Each agency agreed to appoint one member to the new committee with Al Rose, the former chair of the chamber's subcommittee, serving as the seventh member and chairman. The Riverbanks Park Study Committee was instructed to report back to the entire group in the fall, with a recommendation on how the park could be developed. By establishing this committee, the local governments had now effectively taken control of what had so far been a private-sector initiative managed by the Greater Columbia Chamber of Commerce.

To reflect the regional nature of the proposed park, the seven-member Riverbank Park study committee was soon expanded to twelve. Committee members included

the voters of Richland and Lexington Counties to choose between the Riverbanks and Hampton-Preston sites for the Tricentennial exhibit.

Less than a week later, five local governments—the Richland and Lexington legislative delegations, the City of Columbia, the Richland County Board of Administrators, and the Richland Rural Recreation Commission—joined with the Greater Columbia Chamber of Commerce to establish yet another new committee to study the

Al Rose, Greater Columbia Chamber
  chairman
Bud Antley, West Columbia-Cayce Chamber
Edward T. Williams, Lexington County
  Rural Recreation Commission
Jarvis Klapman and Anne Decell, Lexington
  County Delegation
Linwood Shull, Lexington County Board of
  Commissioners
Claire Randall, Richland County Rural Rec-
  reation Commission
Stan Huguenin, Greater Columbia Chamber
  of Commerce

J. Watson Wharton, Richland County Board
    of Administrators
Carey Burnett, Columbia city manager
John Campbell, Columbia City Council
Travis Medlock, Richland County Legisla-
    tive Delegation

The new committee met on August 22 to
review the brief history of the Riverbanks
Park project. Like the chamber's original
subcommittee, the new group decided to
exclude the sixteen-acre Columbia Zoo
property from their deliberations. The
members of the group established a
100,000-dollar budget for Phase I of the
project and discussed operational responsibility. They felt that a multigovernmental
agency would pose too many problems and
hoped that one of the local governments
would step forward and offer to operate
the park. The meeting concluded with a
committee decision to meet with the Richland and Lexington county legislative delegations, Richland's and Lexington's County
Boards of Administrators, and the City of
Columbia in order to present their recommendations.

Two weeks later Claire Randall, representing the Richland County Recreation
Commission, distributed to the committee
a proposed master plan for the Riverbanks
Park. The group agreed that the Richland

County Rural Recreation Commission
should be the administering agency and
that the two counties and the City of
Columbia—and any other interested
local governments—fund the capital and
operating budgets of the park on a per
capita basis.

On September 24, an article in the *State*
suggested that the Riverbanks Park Study
Committee might face legal and political
consequences as a result of their recommendation that the Richland County
Rural Recreation Commission build and
operate a park that would lie partially
within Lexington County. The piece stated
that "There was at least the possibility that

The Riverbanks Park Master Plan included projections that the Columbia Zoo would draw 750,000 visitors in the first year.

The arctic fox was one of the first animals encountered by guests when the zoo opened in 1974.

the Legislature would enter the picture as it did to create Columbia Metropolitan Airport." This was a perceptive and prescient statement, since the legislature had created a special purpose district to develop and administer Columbia's airport. The timing of the park project was also mentioned. With a general election looming in November, some committee members were quoted as saying that the park might become a "political football." Columbia's mayor, Lester Bates, disagreed, saying, "If we get this thing rolling, I'm sure the legal experts can find some way to get it okayed. I don't think we ought to waste any more time."

Nearly a week later, the Richland County Legislative Delegation adopted a resolution asking that the Riverbanks Park Study Committee meet with the South Carolina Department of Parks, Recreation and Tourism to request that the agency consider developing the Riverbanks project. Later that same day, the Richland County Board of Administrators took the opposite approach, by voting to refer the project to the Richland County Rural Recreation Commission, with the stipulation that the commission seek equal financial support from the City of Columbia and Richland and

Lexington Counties. Recreation Commission Chairman Thomas Linton responded by saying that such an agreement was, in his opinion, unconstitutional.

On October 3 Columbia's city manager, Carey Burnett, wrote to Bob Castles of South Carolina Electric and Gas, stating that "it has been decided by the Riverbanks Park Study Committee that the City of Columbia will assume responsibility for the acquisition and development of the Park." Two weeks later the Richland and Lexington legislative delegations sent resolutions to South Carolina Electric and Gas approving the city's lease of the land. A chamber publication stated that the mayor hoped that South Carolina Department of Parks, Recreation and Tourism would at some point take over the park.

Soon after the New Year, in 1969, the City of Columbia decided to move the project forward while the legislative delegations wrestled with the issue of multijurisdictional governance, presumably to be organized along the lines of the governance of the Columbia Metropolitan Airport. The stage was now set. Columbia's zoo was about to become reality.

Caribbean flamingo. One of Riverbanks' original flamingos, #SJ0034, arrived at Riverbanks on September 20, 1973, and still resides at the zoo today. Photograph by Larry Cameron.

Chapter 2

TURNING A DREAM INTO REALITY

Community persistence for the Riverbanks Park continued, and in April 1969 a bill was introduced to the state legislature to create the South Carolina Riverbanks Parks Commission. The bill passed on June 17, and a few weeks later, on July 11, 1969, Secretary of State O. Frank Thornton swore in the first Riverbanks Parks Commission: Donald F. Barton and Lawrence W. Johnson, City of Columbia; Alan P. Rose and Clarence P. Sexton, Lexington County; Joseph C. Good and G. Fred Muller, Richland County; and Norman J. Arnold, at-large/Zoological Society; however, the South Carolina Supreme Court later ruled that a private, nonprofit

organization such as the Zoological Society could not be represented on a public body. Thus Arnold was given the designation of at-large member without reference to any of the three governing bodies. The seven-member team was charged with developing the park and would serve as the governing body of the Rich-Lex Riverbanks Park District, which ultimately was to be known by all as Riverbanks Zoo and Garden.

With the creation of Riverbanks as a special purpose district, the state legislature significantly expanded the zoo's support base. Richland and Lexington Counties joined the City of Columbia

(facing) Riverbanks acquired this pair of wreathed hornbills in the fall of 2011. Photograph by Larry Cameron.

Amur tiger. Photograph by Richard Rokes.

An original rendering of the polar bear exhibit by Gil Petroff.

as full partners in the burgeoning River-banks project. Approximately one hundred acres of land covering both sides of the Lower Saluda River were leased to the commission by South Carolina Electric and Gas for ninety-nine years at one dollar per year.

Shortly after its creation, the River-banks Park Commission began to search for someone to lead them in their quest to build Columbia's first real zoo. As expected, a flood of applications soon arrived, and, after reviewing the assembled résumés, two

top candidates emerged. It is interesting to note that both had backgrounds as reptile experts. At the end of the interview process, the commission chose John Mehrtens to be its first executive director.

The Zoo's First Leader

Riverbanks Zoo and Garden would certainly not exist in its present form were it not for the efforts of John Mehrtens. Brash and bold, Mehrtens almost single-handedly transformed what was to be a small collection of mostly domestic animals and native

Without question Riverbanks owes its success to those dedicated individuals who have served as members of the Riverbanks Park Commission, the zoo and garden's governing authority. Standing mostly in the background, these unsung heroes are the steady hand that guides the ship.

Created by an act of the South Carolina General Assembly in 1969, the commission comprised just seven members, two each representing Richland and Lexington Counties and the City of Columbia and a seventh at-large member rotated among the three governing councils. The commission is responsible to the taxpayers of Richland and Lexington Counties for developing and managing Riverbanks Zoo and Garden in a professional and fiscally responsible manner. They accomplish this mostly by managing the organization's long-range plan and setting policy. Their actions are then carried out through the professional staff.

It is the relationship between the commission and staff that has served Riverbanks and the Midlands so well over the years. Managing the day-to-day operations of a large zoological park and botanical garden requires a variety of special skills, a fact clearly recognized by the commission. From its inception, the commission has fostered the development of a top-notch staff and trusts them to manage the zoo and garden in a professional manner. This is quite rare in the world of nonprofit cultural institutions and stands as the centerpiece of Riverbanks' success.

As of 2013, the current Riverbanks Park Commission comprises Earl F. Brown, Jr., chair; M. F. "Phil" Bartlett, vice chair; Mary Howard, treasurer; Bud Tibshrany, secretary; Lloyd S. Liles; James E. Smith; and Jan Stamps, immediate past chair.

Satch Krantz, Riverbanks' president and CEO, was first hired by John Mehrtens as Columbia Zoo's supervisor of service buildings in 1971.

wildlife into a zoological park of international prominence. However, though he is appropriately credited with creating a great zoo, his personality and management style nearly led to its premature demise.

A native of the Bronx in New York, Mehrtens was a big man with an authoritative presence. He had an excellent command of the English language, and when he walked into a room, people took notice. One of his greatest attributes was his ability to entertain with colorful and descriptive stories about his life in the zoo business. While the facts surrounding many of these stories were often embellished, they fascinated Columbia's political and business leaders.

Mehrtens had a lifelong fascination with reptiles. As a child he hung around the Bronx Zoo reptile house, pestering the keepers with questions about the snakes, lizards, and turtles housed there. He worked in the Cleveland and Columbus zoos in Ohio, first as reptile keeper and later as curator.

His big career break came when he joined the staff of the Fort Worth Zoo in Texas as general curator, but, following a tumultuous stint there, he was later hired to build a zoo in the small town of Victoria, Texas. Frustrated with the pace of getting that zoo off the ground, Mehrtens responded to an ad for a similar position in Columbia, South

Embroidered clothing patch. The zoo's first logo was designed by Doris Mehrtens, wife of Director John Mehrtens.

Carolina, and was soon hired as the director of the new Columbia Zoological Park.

From the beginning Mehrtens was intimately involved in practically every detail surrounding the design, construction, and operation of the Columbia Zoo. The local firm Blume, Cannon, and Ott had been selected as the zoo's official architect and performed admirably under the guidance of the chief designer, Bob Cannon. At the time only a handful of American architects had designed a zoo from scratch, so the road to achievement was wide open. With Mehrtens's vision leading the way, the firm

was sometimes challenged by his exhaustive management style.

Mehrtens was driven to build what he often referred to as a "professional zoo," no matter what the cost. No detail escaped his attention. He struggled to articulate his ideas for the appearance of the big-cat exhibits and on more than one occasion directed the gunite contractor to tear down days of work that didn't meet Mehrtens's expectations. Furthermore his involvement wasn't limited to construction. He even selected the keepers' uniforms (custom-made safari suits that were rarely worn) and formulated the individual diet of every animal in the zoo.

While it had been anticipated that the entire zoo could be built on a budget of $3.3 million, funded with the issuance of general obligation bonds, this proved to be insufficient. Attempts by the commission to control spending were met with opposition, and the commission was forced to ask the local governments for an additional $2.75 million in February 1973, just a year before opening. The request for additional funds

(top) Columbia zoo's first director, John Mehrtens, taking famed TV personality Marlin Perkins around the construction site. (bottom) Construction of the original flamingo exhibit.

met considerable resistance by local leaders but was ultimately approved. The fight over the additional money would prove to be just the beginning of a financial nightmare that would plague the zoo for the next seven years.

Despite all his blunders, Mehrtens was a visionary. While some of his initial ideas resulted in serious design flaws, he instituted several unique and innovative concepts such as underwater viewing for polar bears. He was also a futurist. As early as during the mid-1970s, he predicted, with uncanny accuracy, how zoos would operate in the future.

Mehrtens must also be credited with Riverbanks' ultimate success. Had he not insisted that the zoo be professionally designed and operated, Columbia would likely have been home to a small children's zoo stocked with white-tailed deer and cows. He spoke so eloquently of eagles soaring above the cliffs of the canyon exhibit in the Birdhouse or of Kodiak bears swatting live salmon from a frothing stream in their exhibit that everyone believed it was all possible.

Building a zoo from scratch is a daunting task, even under the best of circumstances. Thousands of details must be addressed,

(top) John Mehrtens accepting a generous donation from students at a local school. (bottom) An original rendering of Ape Island, the concept is much like that of today's Sky-High Safari vertical ropes course for humans.

RIVERBANKS ZOO AND GARDEN

(left) Construction of the original entrance. (right) One of the most active and curious animals in today's Riverbanks collection, this young Hamadryas baboon, Yara, was born at the zoo in November 2010. Photograph by Richard W. Rokes.

from how different animals are to be housed and exhibited to the amenities needed to accommodate hundreds of thousands of visitors. John Mehrtens insisted that he be personally involved in every one of these decisions, no matter how small or mundane. And it didn't help matters that it rained heavily at nearly every critical point in the construction process. As a result building the zoo took longer than originally planned.

Building an Ark

Zoos and aquariums acquire individual animals on a regular basis, but in the past forty years there have only been three zoos—

Riverbanks Zoo, North Carolina Zoo, and Minnesota Zoo—that have been built from scratch and thus have required an entire collection of animals. In the months leading up to Columbia Zoo's opening, animals arrived on an almost daily basis; sometimes just one or two, other times by the truckload. The largest of these shipments was on a caravan of trucks that arrived from a Miami animal dealer and carried, among other things, tigers, leopards, hippos, wallabies, African-crested porcupines, and baboons. The arrival of the animals was complicated. Much of the zoo was still under construction, and few roads and sidewalks were paved. The staff

TURNING A DREAM INTO REALITY

he had been wrongly terminated, and, without him at the helm, the zoo was doomed to fail. He then asked that area residents contact local and state government authorities and demand that he be immediately reinstated.

His claims disrupted the efforts of the commission and staff to get the zoo on an even political keel. In response the commission contacted the then-named American Association of Zoological Parks and Aquariums (AAZPA; now the AZA) for advice. Bob Wagner, at the time the AAZPA executive director, had the perfect solution. He suggested that the commission engage the services of Charles Schroeder, the recently retired director of the Zoological Society of San Diego. Schroeder was an international zoo icon, who had almost single-handedly established the San Diego Zoo as one of the world's great zoological parks.

Not only had Schroeder just retired, he also was in the early stages of establishing himself as a zoo consultant. In early June the commission hired him to serve as Riverbanks' acting executive director, but in reality he was charged with two specific duties: quell the rumors that were being spread by John Mehrtens and serve as a one-man search committee for Riverbanks' next director. With Schroeder assuming the

Did You Know?

Satch Krantz is one of only three American zoo directors who have served as president of both the Association of Zoos and Aquariums (AZA) and the World Association of Zoos & Aquariums (WAZA)—and the first zoo director to serve two presidential terms for AZA since WWII.

title of acting director, Krantz was assigned a new title as assistant director. His temporary reign over Riverbanks lasted less than eight weeks.

Schroeder arrived in Columbia on Monday, June 21, 1976. Chairman Barton greeted him at the airport and drove him directly to the zoo. Krantz and Schroeder met for the first time just inside the front gate. Schroeder had a well-deserved reputation for being honest and forthright, and when he spoke about zoos, the entire profession listened. His mere presence in Columbia spoke volumes to zoo professionals and local residents alike—this was a community that cared deeply about its new zoo and Mehrtens's diatribe against the commission soon subsided.

With the Mehrtens issue behind him, Schroeder turned his attention to hiring Riverbanks' next executive director. He needed

Dr. Charles Schroeder, the recently retired director of the San Diego Zoo, acted as a one-man search committee to identify Riverbanks' second director. He recommended Satch Krantz, who was just twenty-six years old at the time, and sent this congratulatory letter after he was hired.

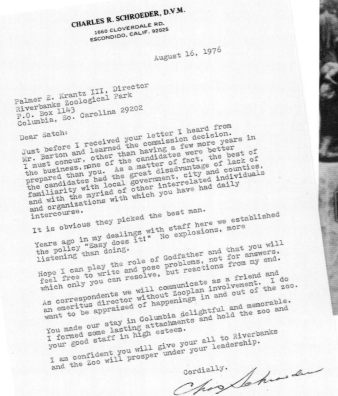

CHARLES R. SCHROEDER, D.V.M.
1660 CLOVERDALE RD.
ESCONDIDO, CALIF. 92025

August 16, 1976

Palmer E. Krantz III, Director
Riverbanks Zoological Park
P.O. Box 1143
Columbia, So. Carolina 29202

Dear Satch:

Just before I received your letter I heard from Mr. Barton and learned the commission decision. I must concur, other than having a few more years in the business, none of the candidates were better prepared than you. As a matter of fact, the best of the candidates had the great disadvantage of lack of familiarity with local government, city and counties, and with the myriad of other interrelated individuals and organizations with which you have had daily intercourse.

It is obvious they picked the best man.

Years ago in my dealings with staff here we established the policy "Easy does it!" No explosions, more listening than doing.

Hope I can play the role of Godfather and that you will feel free to write and pose problems, not for answers, which only you can resolve, but reactions from my end.

As correspondents we will communicate as a friend and an emeritus director without Zooplan involvement. I do want to be appraised of happenings in and out of the zoo.

You made our stay in Columbia delightful and memorable. I formed some lasting attachments and hold the zoo and your good staff in high esteem.

I am confident you will give your all to Riverbanks and the Zoo will prosper under your leadership.

Cordially,

Chas Schroeder

Satch Krantz (right) confers with Dr. Charles Schroeder (left) during his visit to Riverbanks.

only to place an ad in the monthly publication of the AAZPA to generate a qualified list of candidates. Twenty-two people applied for the position, and from these he chose to interview only two. The top candidate was the assistant director of a larger zoo, but, after visiting Columbia, he withdrew his name from consideration. The number two candidate, the experienced director of a large midwestern zoo, was offered the job but declined it when he and the commission were unable to agree on a salary.

During this time Krantz continued to oversee the day-to-day operation of the zoo, confident that Schroeder would find a highly qualified person to take over the reigns. Immediately after negotiations with the second candidate fell through, Schroeder approached Krantz and asked for a copy of his résumé. He wanted him to apply for the position. Not having one at hand, Krantz scribbled what had to be the most unimpressive résumé ever written, and on a single piece of lined notebook paper at that.

Schroeder left Columbia on July 28, just a month after first arriving. In his final report to the commission, Schroeder made several suggestions for improving the zoo, including that the commission build several exhibits for North American animals on its land across the Saluda River and connect them to the existing zoo by aerial gondola. He concluded his report by recommending that the commission hire Krantz to be its next executive director. On August 7, 1976, the commission voted unanimously to offer Krantz the position. Five days later he accepted at an annual salary of $18,000.

Commission Chairman Barton submitted his resignation at that same meeting. After seven years of shepherding the zoo through construction and opening and all the challenges and conflicts, he was understandably ready to call it quits. The ultimate statesman, he also acknowledged his desire to see Krantz start anew, with a fresh chairman.

John Mehrtens

John Mehrtens left Columbia in the fall of 1976 and worked briefly as a consultant with a zoo design firm before landing a position with the Minnesota State Zoo that did not involve managing animals. The zoo was then under construction. He left the position just a few months later and soon moved to the Jackson-

Mehrtens's drive turned a small children's zoo into a major zoological park.

ville Zoo in Florida, where he worked on a master plan for that facility. After a year he moved further south to Miami, where he found work as a sales representative for an animal importer. Other than his brief stints at the Minnesota and Jacksonville zoos, he never worked in a zoo again. Mehrtens died on June 20, 1988. He was just sixty years old.

At the conclusion of the meeting, Riverbanks Zoo had a new director, and the commission had a new chairman, banker Lawrence W. Johnson.

Krantz would later say that had he been a little older and wiser he would never have accepted the commission's offer. He knew nothing about the business end of the zoo.

Like much of the zoo at the time, the original waterfowl exhibit (now the site of the Bird Conservation Center) featured a red-and-black Oriental theme.

and I walked into the council chamber, we were met with the unmistakable sights and sounds of flashbulbs and clicking camera shutters. I turned and looked back towards the door, curious to see who was garnering all the media attention. Seeing no one there, I suddenly realized that all of the photographic and television cameras were pointed directly at me. I was exhilarated, shocked, and embarrassed all at the same time."

Solving the Financial Crisis

With new leadership in place, the first order of business was to remove the zoo from the front page of the newspapers. Riverbanks had been plagued by negative publicity for much of the previous two years. It was now time to bring the zoo's budget under control.

Balance sheets and budgets were completely foreign to him, and he had never dealt with a serious personnel issue or met one-on-one with a politician or donor. Amazingly, in those past 12 months he had served as the zoo's general curator, acting codirector, acting director, acting assistant director, acting director again and finally executive director. Most impressive of all, he was also the youngest zoo director in the United States.

Krantz has told the following story as evidence of his naïveté. "A week after accepting the commission's job offer, arrangements were made for me to make a brief introductory appearance before Columbia City Council. As Don Barton

Cutting expenses proved to be easy. With a total budget of only $1.15 million, even the smallest reduction in expenses produced dramatic results. First on the chopping block was the animal food budget, which had risen steadily despite the fact that the size of the animal collection had remained stable. Six months after Mehrtens's departure, the animal food budget was reduced by $100,000, effectively cutting it in half. Another twenty years would pass before the food budget would again reach the 1976 level. By that time the animal collection had more than tripled.

Further savings were achieved by reducing the zoo's staff. This too proved to be relatively painless. The level of excitement and enthusiasm associated with building the zoo had passed, producing an emotional letdown for many. Operating the zoo on a day-to-day basis was just not the same as creating waterfalls and rain forests. Replacing lightbulbs and changing air filters did not have the same appeal as moving tigers and elephants. The opening of the zoo, combined with the financial crisis and Mehrtens's dismissal, caused many employees to leave.

Many of these positions were simply not replaced. For example, the art department had swollen to include fourteen employees in the final year of construction. These workers were used in a variety of ways, from producing interpretive graphics and brochures to constructing fiberglass waterfalls and cork bark trees in the Ecosystem Birdhouse. With the zoo now open, many of these skills were no longer needed.

The cuts had an immediate and positive impact on the zoo's relationship with its local-government funding partners. The commission and staff were making tough decisions in an effort to become more fiscally responsible, and local political leaders responded by scaling back their fiery rhetoric. This did not mean that the zoo's

One of a handful of zoos that successfully breeds Toco toucans each year, Riverbanks has fledged twenty-nine Toco toucan chicks over the past ten years. Keepers will assist the parents as needed by supplementing the chicks' diet to assure that these vibrant, curious young birds continue to grow and entertain guests for years to come. Photograph by Richard W. Rokes.

financial woes were over. For the next couple of years, the zoo would suffer from a lack of a stable funding strategy.

The Making of a Millage Agency

In spite of many cost saving initiatives, the zoo continued to struggle financially. Richland and Lexington Counties along with the City of Columbia had promised to fund the zoo's operations equally through opening day. After that the park was to be self-sufficient. But, regardless of how much expenses were cut, operating costs continued to exceed earned revenues. The only way the zoo was able to survive during this critical time was through the generosity of the three local governments and the patience and understanding of major suppliers.

The two counties and the city found themselves in a conundrum. On the one hand, they were still angry with the zoo for what they perceived to be an irresponsible promise of self-sufficiency and grossly inflated attendance and revenue projections. In the minds of these government leaders, they were being asked to continue contributing precious tax dollars for a project they never asked for, much less approved. The only means of expressing their displeasure

Grant's zebra, aptly named Milly. Photograph by Larry Cameron.

was by questioning the zoo's continuing need for operating support. This strategy often backfired, since voters loved the new zoo. The paradox led to yet another political battleground.

Absent of any kind of binding agreement between 1974 and 1980, a matching amount was requested of each of the major local governments each year. And each year one or more of the governments would withhold some of the amount requested, causing the zoo to tighten its fiscal belt even more.

When questioned by reporters about their votes, members of the councils would find it necessary to criticize the zoo. This invariably led to an avalanche of letters to the editor and editorials taking them to task for not fully funding the wonderful new zoo. Once again the zoo was the white elephant.

In the summer of 1976, members of the Lexington Board of County Commissioners decided they had had enough. They decided to put the future of the zoo in the hands of their constituents by holding a nonbinding referendum in conjunction with that year's general election.

Even more important to note, the election would also result in a reconstituted county government, as Lexington County voters would elect their first council under the new Home Rule Act. Prior to 1975

(top) Bird keeper Jennifer Jeffcoat feeding members of the zoo's original jackass penguin colony. (bottom) Visitors take in the original hippo exhibit. Note the steel handrails and lack of vegetation.

Riverbanks has gained an international reputation for breeding rare and endangered animals, including the highly endangered black rhinoceros.

South Carolina's counties were basically run by their respective legislative delegations. That year the General Assembly passed the Home Rule Act, which implemented specific changes in the state constitution, and as a result the powers of county councils were significantly expanded. For the first time in history, county councils could actually control the destiny of their county and citizenry.

In addition to helping choose a new U.S. president and a county council, when Lexington County residents entered the voting booths on November 2, 1976, they were asked to vote yes or no on the following question: "Do you favor the levy of a general ad valorem property tax of two (2) mills in Lexington County for the purpose of providing operational support to the Riverbanks Park Commission?" There has probably never been a more loaded question in the history of South Carolina politics.

Rather than providing the new council with a clear direction on the zoo's future, the election only added to the confusion. Each council member was actually elected to serve one of nine new districts. When the referendum votes were tallied along district lines, the measure failed—with five districts voting to cease funding the zoo and four voting in favor. However, the measure barely passed by a popular vote, of 17,155 to 15,829, with the more urban districts voting overwhelmingly to support the zoo.

Four of the newly elected council members, Sonny Dubose, Jerry Howard, Russell Shealy, and Butch Spires, were forward-thinking young men suddenly faced with interpreting the results of the referendum. To their collective credit, they decided that the popular vote took precedent over the district vote and declared a narrow victory for the zoo.

But they did more than that. With a background in marketing, Sonny Dubose contacted the marketing department at the University of South Carolina and convinced them to do a study of the zoo. They concluded that with its strong support among the general public, a private, nonprofit support organization could potentially generate substantial financial resources. This conclusion would soon be validated with a revamped Riverbanks Society.

Soon thereafter members of Lexington County Council met with their counterparts from Richland County and the City of Columbia. The topic was clear—the zoo "crisis" had become divisive to the

Spectacled bear cub. Over the years Riverbanks has hosted a number of promotional events including a teddy-bear rally celebrating the arrival of South America's only bear.

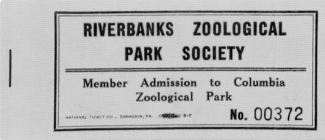

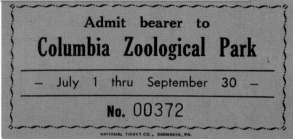

The original Riverbanks Society pass gave members free admission for one visit for each of the four seasons of the year.

entire Midlands community and had to be addressed in a responsible and meaningful way. Out of this meeting a plan was developed. In 1981 the Richland and Lexington County Councils would begin funding the zoo as a millage agency, thus guaranteeing the financial support needed to adequately fund the operating budget. As a result of this agreement, the City of Columbia dropped out as a funding partner because city residents also pay county taxes and could not be "double-dipped" for the same service.

The zoo's funding crisis ended at the stroke of midnight on June 30, 1980,

the official end of the 1979–80 fiscal year. The bold decision to assess the taxpayers of Richland and Lexington Counties as a means of supplementing the operating budget was perhaps just as important as the decision to build the zoo in the first place. With a steady and reliable source of operating revenue, the commission and staff could for the first time turn their attention to the future. In some respects this could be termed the real beginning of Riverbanks Zoo and Garden.

Community Support

Despite the various controversies surrounding the new zoo, its popularity continued to grow, and local citizens began asking how they could help. The staff chose a proven method of fulfilling their generous offer. Most successful zoos utilize nonprofit membership organizations as one means of garnering public support and contributions. Known by names such as Friends of the National Zoo or North Carolina Zoological Society, these organizations followed a fairly well-defined formula; in return for an annual fee, members receive unlimited free admission to the zoo, a monthly publication, and discounts at the gift shop and snack bars. Mehrtens had toyed with this concept, but, as previously mentioned, instead of awarding unlimited free admission, the zoo

TURNING A DREAM INTO REALITY

offered members just one free pass in each of the four seasons: summer, fall, winter, and spring. This concept proved to be unpopular and managed to enroll only a few hundred members.

The staff pitched the concept for a reamped society in 1976. With the commission's support and encouragement, a telephone survey was conducted of similar-sized zoos, and within a few short months the Riverbanks Society was reestablished.

Following a brainstorming session one afternoon, the zoo staff approached the City of Columbia with a rather unorthodox request. Would the city be willing to place a society membership application in their monthly water bills? The thought was that this would be the quickest and least expensive means of getting applications into the hands of Columbia-area residents. With the city's blessing, the forms were printed, and, within days of the mailing, a few completed applications began to trickle into the zoo office. The trickle quickly turned into a flood, and in a few weeks more than two thousand applications from throughout Richland and Lexington Counties had been received.

The significance of the society's founding and subsequent success cannot be overstated. Politicians could never again say that their

A Fine Champion

More than forty years later, the first chairman of Riverbanks Park Commission, Don Barton, remains one of Riverbanks' greatest supporters and still serves the zoo ex officio as director emeritus on today's board of directors of Riverbanks Society.

One of many celebrities to visit Riverbanks as a guest speaker for the Riverbanks Society, Amanda Blake, who played "Miss Kitty" on the TV show Gunsmoke, watches the zoo's cheetahs.

Keeper Deborah Elgin feeds Montgomery the hippo. Montgomery was born at the Memphis Zoo on September 17, 1972, and was among the first animals on display when the zoo opened 1974. He resided at Riverbanks until his death in July 2008.

constituents did not support the new zoo or that it was an unwanted burden on taxpayers. The society continued its phenomenal growth throughout the 1980s and 1990s, and, by the time Riverbanks celebrated its thirtieth anniversary in 2003, membership had peaked with more than thirty-five thousand households in the Midlands and beyond.

A True Partnership

It's hard to imagine Riverbanks Zoo and Garden without Riverbanks Society. Since its inception in 1976, the society, a state-chartered nonprofit organization, has been a full and enthusiastic partner in the success of the zoo and garden. It's little wonder that political and business leaders constantly refer to the relationship between the Riverbanks Society and the Riverbanks Park Commission as the ultimate private/ public partnership.

Starting with a base of just a few hundred memberships, Riverbanks Society now boasts more than thirty-three thousand annual household memberships and is one of the largest zoo-support organizations on a per capita basis in the United States. President and CEO Satch Krantz frequently refers to the zoo and garden's funding base as a three-legged stool—the three legs represent earned revenue, local government support and the Riverbanks Society. In addition to contributing $1 million a year to the zoo and garden's general fund budget, the society has raised additional millions for capital improvements.

Riverbanks Society is managed by a volunteer board of directors. These dedicated public servants represent a cross-section

The Single Largest Bequest

In November 2011 Riverbanks Society received the single largest bequest in the zoo's forty-year history—an $863,000 unrestricted gift from the Charitable Remainder Trust of Melinda Poole Grizzell, a longtime, dedicated supporter of Riverbanks. The gift came at a critical point in the zoo's history, as capital improvement needs had increased and no major new exhibits had been added in the previous ten years.

of the Midlands community—from bank executives and attorneys to educators and community activists. No matter what their background or professional affiliation, they are all motivated by one factor—a love of Riverbanks Zoo and Garden.

(overleaf) African elephant. Photograph by Larry Cameron.

Chapter 3

PICKING UP MOMENTUM

Riverbanks Zoo received a major public relations boost when the December 1976 issue of *Family Circle* hit newsstands. The magazine included a two-page article titled "A Zoo's Who," by Jean Anderson, and this changed forever how Columbians felt about their new zoo. The piece was really nothing more than a subjective compilation of the thirteen "best" zoos in the United States. Almost all America's major zoos made the list, including the Bronx and San Diego zoos and the National Zoo in Washington, D.C. Appearing at number four was the smallest zoo in the smallest city to make the list—the new zoo in Columbia, South Carolina. The description of the Columbia Zoological Park stated, in its entirety: "America's newest zoo (opened in 1974) sprawls along the banks of the boulder-strewn Saluda River. Although

the grounds cover 150 acres, only 50 of them are given over to exhibits (the zoo is developing along a 20-year master plan). Already, however, its Eco-System Birdhouse (80 exhibits with 600 birds representing 150 species) is considered one of the country's finest; it is subdivided into geographic zones—desert, canyon, swamp, seashore and rain forest (twice-daily downpours here with wind, thunder and lightning). Don't miss the polar bear exhibit with its underwater viewing room or the Kalahari Desert lions (the only group of them in America)."

It didn't matter that the article's introduction stated it was based on "personal visits, the preferences and proddings of friends and the recommendations of more than a few zoo people" or that the list was organized geographically and not in the

order of excellence. The *Family Circle* article resonated with the community—Columbia was now home to the fourth best zoo in the United States.

Eight years later, on February 19, 1984, *Parade,* the Sunday newspaper magazine insert, published an article, "Can Zoos Be Humane?" Author Michael Satchell visited fifteen zoos around the United States in an effort to highlight what he considered to be poor conditions found in many American zoos. The piece contained a sidebar titled "The 10 Best and 10 Worst Zoos." The ten best were rated the finest in the nation by an informal poll of zoo professionals. The zoos were listed alphabetically, and there sat Riverbanks once again in the number four spot.

Incredibly, lightning struck not twice, but three times. Riverbanks would be ranked number four again, twenty-eight years later. In the spring of 2012, TripAdvisor, the world's largest travel-related website, ranked Riverbanks number four in its popularity index of the top ten zoos in the United States for its ability to provide guests with up-close animal exhibits and interactive attractions. According to one TripAdvisor traveler, "Riverbanks Zoo is the perfect family outing."

Two of Riverbanks' beloved giraffes. A total of six giraffes have been born at Riverbanks since 2009. Photograph by Ron Brasington.

Topping TripAdvisor's list of top ten zoos was the Henry Doorly Zoo in Omaha, Nebraska, followed by the St. Louis Zoo in Saint Louis, Missouri, and the Cape May County Park and Zoo in Cape May Court House, New Jersey. Behind Riverbanks was the Memphis Zoo in Memphis, Tennessee, and the San Diego Zoo in San Diego, California. Audubon Zoo in New Orleans, Louisiana, rounded out the top ten.

These unsolicited accolades helped create a Columbia urban legend—that there exists an official ranking system, similar to a college football poll, listing the ten best zoos in the United States. In fact such an official poll does not exist, yet Riverbanks has consistently placed fourth in informal ratings.

The Enlightening Eighties

Zoos were undergoing tremendous change in the late 1970s and early 1980s. As the result of a better-educated workforce and an increasingly informed public, zoos began a transformation that in many ways still continues today. Foremost among these was the increasing emphasis on zoos as unique educational resources. It was during this time that Riverbanks hired its first curator of education, a move that led directly to the first expansion of the zoo site, the construction of the Education Center. Prior to the hiring of the curator and the opening

Wild about Riverbanks

"My family & I are members of the zoo. . . . we visited the National Zoo in Washington, DC last week & they don't hold a candle to our Riverbanks Zoo in Columbia . . . . our zoo in Columbia [is] so much more inviting and clean and easy to get around. Thank you for all that you do for our city and our state. We are proud to be members of the Riverbanks Zoo!"

Rob & Kim Johnson, Columbia, S.C.

Schoolchildren meet a boa constrictor during one of the zoo's educational programs.

(top) Breaking ground on the site of the new Education Center, September 29, 1982. (bottom) Longtime curator of birds Bob Seibels shows schoolchildren an ostrich egg.

of the center in 1983, the zoo's education offerings were confined almost exclusively to guided tours of the zoo. These tours were conducted by a dedicated group of volunteers, known as docents. The Education Center was funded exclusively through a private fundraising campaign and featured classrooms, a library, and a 200-seat auditorium allowing the zoo to expand its educational programming greatly as well as serve as an additional resource to the community for meetings, lectures, and films.

Bolstered by the growing popularity of the zoo as well as the success of the society, the commission and staff began to seriously consider Riverbanks' first major expansion. Given the somewhat rocky financial and political roads the zoo had traveled over the past ten years, this was a bold move indeed.

But it was clear that shortcomings of the original zoo, especially those related to guest amenities, had to be corrected. Foremost among these were the undersized front entrance and the lack of an adequate restaurant and gift shop. While the original zoo was basically the product of one man's imagination, the Riverbanks leadership now chose to engage the services of a professional zoo design firm, CLRdesign of Philadelphia.

In the mid-1980s, zoo architecture was beginning to emerge as a specialty when a

In the last ten years, AZA-accredited zoos and aquariums formally trained more than four hundred thousand teachers nationwide, supporting science curricula with effective teaching materials and hands-on opportunities. School field trips connected more than twelve million students with the natural world.

In South Carolina, Riverbanks teamed up with the Boys and Girls Clubs of the Midlands in 2003 to pilot the "Teens in Action" program for underserved teenagers. Designed to connect area teenagers to nature and build successful, caring members of the community and the world, the project originally started with six participants and earned the 2004 Education Award from the Association of Zoos and Aquariums. The program today, aptly named ZooTeens, is managed solely by Riverbanks. Each summer more than thirty-five ZooTeens meet new friends, have fun with peers, and gain valuable life skills that help lead to their success and inspire positive changes in the world.

Whether engaged in day camps, school programs, overnights or behind-the-scenes tours, kids and parents can be certain that Riverbanks' team of highly skilled educators will provide interactive and captivating learning experiences that will keep people coming back for more. Annually more than 100 Boy Scouts and Girl Scouts earn badges and try-its during Scout Saturdays; about 300 homeschoolers explore a range of topics in Homeschool Mondays; nearly 650 guests get an inside look at some out-of-sight places during behind-the-scenes Adventure Tours; more than 1,000 campers meet new friends and create wild summer memories at Zoo Camp; around 2,500 visitors spend the night during the zoo's overnight programs; and nearly 8,000 students take part in the zoo's inquiry-based school programs, designed to meet South Carolina science academic standards.

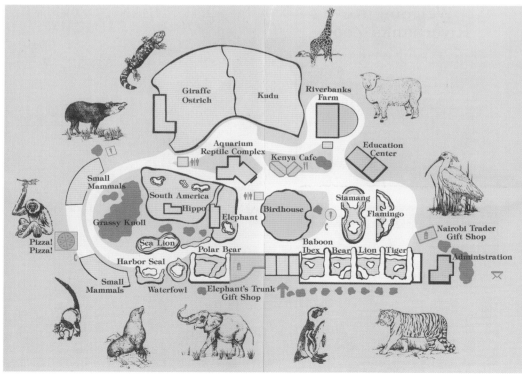

Giraffe
Ostrich

Kudu

Riverbanks
Farm

Aquarium
Reptile Complex

Kenya Cafe

Education
Center

Small
Mammals

South America

Hippo

Elephant

Birdhouse

Siamang

Flamingo

Grassy Knoll

Sea Lion

Polar Bear

Baboon
Ibex Bear Lion Tiger

Nairobi Trader
Gift Shop

Pizza!
Pizza!

Harbor Seal

Administration

Small
Mammals

Waterfowl

Elephant's Trunk
Gift Shop

Contorted Mulberry—*Morus alba* 'Unryu'

COLOR: Green foliage.

BLOOMING PERIOD: Grown for winter structure

TYPE: Deciduous tree

SIZE: 15 to 20 feet tall if cut back to the ground every few years

EXPOSURE: Full Sun

Photograph by Andy Cabe.

What a fun plant! Large leaves and contorted stems make this shrub a quirky addition to the garden. Although contorted mulberry can reach 20 feet, the staff at Riverbanks prefers to cut the shrub to the ground each February to encourage more curls in the woody stems. This is a plant that just keeps giving. Use the cut stems as decoration in your garden by embellishing them with spray paint. For a glimpse of a great stand of mulberry, check out Fort Mulberry at Riverbanks Botanical Garden.

(left, clockwise) Riverbanks offers free admission to K–12 students attending Richland and Lexington county schools on school-approved field trips. A family gets up close to a Galapagos tortoise during one of the zoo's Adventure Tours. Photograph by Robin Vondrak Photography. Volunteer diver in the Indo-Pacific Coral Reef tank. Visitors can watch a diver feed the fish at 12:30 P.M. daily in the Aquarium-Reptile Complex. Photograph by Richard W. Rokes. Zoo map c. 1990.

(overleaf, clockwise) Tonight Show regular and San Diego Zoo's "Goodwill Ambassador" Joan Embrey visits with an elephant. Embrey was guest speaker at Riverbanks' tenth anniversary celebration. The golden poison dart frog is considered one of the most toxic animals on the planet. Photograph by Larry Cameron. The area now occupied by the gorilla exhibit was originally known as the Grassy Knoll and served as the location of numerous special events for many years.

Our family has enjoyed Riverbanks Zoo & Garden since 1988 when we moved to West Columbia from Ohio. We were fortunate to live nearby and when the garden entrance was opened we would just walk from the house to spend the day there.

My husband was deployed three times while we lived there with each deployment lasting 12 to 15 months so I would take our young son to Riverbanks quite a bit. He enjoyed seeing all the amazing animals and cool flowers and walking along the trails. . . . It was a great way to pass the time during those long months.

Over the years our son participated in the many programs offered by Riverbanks from constructing a scarecrow to planting grass in Easter baskets to learning how to care for ponies. His favorite was the summer camp program where they got to go out and kayak.

One of my favorite Riverbanks memories is when my husband volunteered at the aquarium by getting into his scuba gear and going into the large tank to feed the fish. I brought our son to see him and he was so excited that his dad was in there that he would proudly tell every visitor who came by, "That's my dad! See that man? That's my dad!!"

Our son is a young man now and shortly before we were transferred to another state we had an engraved brick placed in the zoo in honor of my husband's military service. And fittingly it is right outside the aquarium entrance!

Riverbanks Zoo & Garden has been a very special place for us and means a lot to our family. We wish to thank you for all the wonderful animal exhibits, educational opportunities, and the inspiring gardening ideas we've enjoyed over the years.

Tracey Baker, Lillington, N.C.—Riverbanks member, 1998–2011

The zoo's original Halloween Spooktacular debuted in the late 1980s. While the event drew big crowds like the one pictured here, it was discontinued after a few years due to logistics issues.

handful of firms around the United States began devoting the majority of their practices to the design of zoo exhibits. The discipline of zoo design grew from a series of exhibits at the Woodland Park Zoo in Seattle, Washington, that utilized a concept known as landscape immersion. Traditional zoo exhibits typically featured well-defined lines between visitor and animal, using concrete sidewalks, steel handrails, and contrived rows of ornamental shrubs and flowers. (Riverbanks' five original grottos for big cats and bears were typical of this school of design.) By contrast the landscape immersion concept intentionally blurred that line by using curving sidewalks, strategically placed

"viewing windows," and heavy landscaping that, in most instances, mimicked the animal's native habitat.

Working with the zoo staff, the architects (a partnership between CLR and LS3P of Charleston) developed an entirely new guest services plan, requiring the relocation and expansion of the main entrance, complete with a greatly enlarged gift shop and the addition of a sit-down restaurant. Recognizing that ticket booths and eateries lack a certain amount of appeal, especially to the politicians who would decide the fate of the expansion effort, the zoo staff added three additional projects that were proven crowd-pleasers: an aquarium, a reptile house, and a children's farm.

Armed with an exciting new $6.35 million plan (dubbed Zoo II), the commission began discussions with Richland and Lexington County Councils regarding a bond issue in 1986. Despite reservations by some Lexington County Council members that the plan again excluded expansion into their county, the bond issue was approved.

With funding secured, the Riverbanks design team began the process of developing the details of Zoo II. As a result of this process, the proposed aquarium and reptile house were combined into a single exhibit, called the Aquarium-Reptile Complex (ARC). Riverbanks Farm, Kenya Café,

STATUS—Coral reefs (relatives of jellies and sea anemones) are under stress throughout the world. Threats such as climate change, runoff pollution, overfishing, and disease are causing massive coral deaths. It is believed that 10 percent of the coral reefs worldwide are already dead.

WHERE IN THE WORLD—Reef-building corals are found only in the photic zone (down to 50 meters, as far as sunlight can penetrate) and only in clear tropical waters between the Tropic of Cancer and Tropic of Capricorn.

ON THE MENU—Corals can feed both by autotrophy and heterotrophy. This means they can feed themselves (by capturing light energy) and get food from external sources (capturing small plankton as it floats by). In the aquarium, corals receive both types of food sources. Corals at the zoo dine on home-grown plankton several times a day, and they also take in specialty lighting that replicates the intensity and wavelength of sunlight.

Trumpet coral. In an effort to help ensure the future of wild coral reefs, Riverbanks' aquarists propagate corals such as the trumpet coral pictured here on-site at the zoo. Photograph by Larry Cameron.

CLAIM TO FAME—Tourism. Coral reefs have become popular tourist destinations, attracting snorkelers and divers for the sheer diversity of animal life that call the reef "home." Although coral reef ecosystems are found in only .1 percent of the world's ocean surface, nearly 25 percent of all marine animals live on reefs. This incredible biodiversity is what makes corals and coral reefs famous.

AMAZING ADAPTATION—Corals are sessile animals, meaning they cannot move around to escape predators. Instead they have stinging cells called nematocycts that they use for protection. These tiny harpoonlike cells can inject venom into anything that brushes up against the coral, delivering a nasty sting.

COOL CHARACTERISTICS—Many reef-building corals can reproduce asexually. This means that a parent colony can be cut into smaller pieces, and each piece will grow into a new individual colony. Aquaculturists use this mode of reproduction to their advantage in order to grow many, many pieces of coral from only one parent piece.

RIVERBANKS' ROLE—Serving as good stewards of our ocean resources, zoo aquarists pay close attention to the sources of the reef-building corals in the collection. Corals are usually obtained from other public aquariums, donated by local hobbyists, or purchased as aquacultured specimens, rather than collected from the wild. The aquarists at Riverbanks have been successfully culturing corals in the behind-the-scenes area since 1999.

KEEPER'S NOTE—Some corals like to capture plankton to obtain their food. In order to provide it as a food source, phytoplankton and zooplankton are cultured at Riverbanks. While something of a "mad scientist" lab with bubbling green and brown water, this facility is where the food is grown, providing a necessary part of the diet for the living coral reefs.

(top) Governor Carroll Campbell of South Carolina opening Riverbanks Farm in the spring of 1988. (bottom) Children with Blondie the Belgian draft horse, a favorite at the Riverbanks Farm.

and the new entrance and gift shop rounded out the list of Zoo II projects.

Along the way an amazing thing happened. Even though the newly approved projects were still several years away, attendance to the zoo began to grow . . . and grow . . . and grow. In 1990, the year following the completion of the final Zoo II project, one million people visited Riverbanks Zoo. Just three years earlier, attendance stood at 575,000. Even more amazing is the fact that the zoo's attendance would remain near this level for the next twenty-five years. No other North American zoo had ever experienced such a dramatic and sustained growth in attendance.

As the first major project of Zoo II, Riverbanks Farm opened on April 9, 1988. The primary structure of this farm was a 3,500-square-foot wooden barn, home to barn owls, pigs, cows, and Nubian goats. Even though South Carolina is still largely rural in nature, Columbia is a fast-growing city, and many of its youngest residents are as unfamiliar with domestic livestock as their counterparts in New York and Los Angeles. The Riverbanks Farm was designed to explain the methods, as well as the importance, of the farm industry to the state of South Carolina. In addition it allows zoo visitors, especially children, to compare the behavior and management of domestic and exotic animals. In fact, in donating the major gift that made the Riverbanks Farm a reality, Columbia Farms dedicated their commitment to the project to the children of South Carolina.

Clearly the highlight of the Zoo II expansion effort was the Aquarium-Reptile Complex, also known as the ARC. A survey of zoo guests indicated that most visitors wanted to see reptiles, specifically large dangerous snakes, and were keenly interested in an aquarium. Armed with that knowledge, Riverbanks decided to give them both and designed an exceptional exhibit that combined the traditional "reptile house" with an aquarium, all in one facility. The ARC opened in November 1989, boasting a 21,000-square-foot building containing six galleries, a 55,000-gallon Indo-Pacific reef tank, and thousands of individual animals representing hundreds of different species, including some of the most wonderfully beautiful, fascinating, and, in some cases, dangerous animals on the planet. By design the ARC was not intended to be a traditional reptile house or aquarium, but rather a unique blending of the two. The combination of innovative design, fascinating creatures, and creative educational graphics has made the ARC the zoo's most popular exhibit—a distinction it still enjoys today—and earned the exhibit a

Riverbanks appeared on national television when NBC's Today Show personality Willard Scott opened the Aquarium-Reptile Complex in 1989. He returned to Columbia in 1995 to open Riverbanks Botanical Garden.

1990 Significant Achievement Award from the Association of Zoos and Aquariums. Yet no one could have predicted the significant strides in science and conservation that would be made over the years as a direct result of work performed by Riverbanks' ARC biologists.

Capitalizing on Concessions

The sale of food and merchandise within the zoo presents quite a paradox. On the

STATUS—Threatened

WHERE IN THE WORLD—King cobras occupy a huge range stretching from western India, east to the Philippines, and from southern China to Java. Their preferred habitat is bamboo thickets and forests. Riverbanks' king cobras are housed in a large diorama in the Tropical Gallery inside the Aquarium-Reptile Complex; the exhibit portrays the ruin of an ancient Buddhist temple. Look inside the large ceramic pot—it's a favorite lair of the king.

ON THE MENU—As their scientific name suggests, king cobras feed almost exclusively on other snakes in the wild, but keepers train the king cobras at Riverbanks to feed on quail and rodents.

CLAIM TO FAME—Size. King cobras are the largest venomous snakes in the world and can attain lengths of 19 feet. They possess powerful neurotoxic venom and a fierce reputation, but in reality can be quite docile. Some villages have been known to have a "pet" king cobra that is allowed to roam freely and even be handled by children.

AMAZING ADAPTATION—King cobras are among the few snakes that can "vocalize." They possess tracheal diverticula in the upper respiratory tract that function as a low-frequency resonating chamber. When threatened, king cobras will forcibly expel air from their lungs through the diverticula, producing a low frequency growl. When the king growls, one must be especially careful.

COOL CHARACTERISTICS—King cobras are alert and curious and always interested in what the keepers are doing. Reptile keepers have been training the king cobras at Riverbanks to perform rudimentary tasks on command for a food reward.

RIVERBANKS' ROLE—Riverbanks has maintained a colony of king cobras for more than two decades and is one of the few

King cobra. Photograph by Richard W. Rokes.

institutions that breed this species. Baby king cobras hatched at the zoo have been distributed to other zoos around the world.

KEEPER'S NOTE—King cobras are the only snakes that construct an elaborate nest. Usually built of bamboo leaves, the nest has two chambers: one for the eggs and another for the female, who stays close by the nest to protect the incubating eggs. Once the eggs hatch, the baby kings receive no care from the female, who then abandons the nest.

one hand, the funds generated through the sale of food and gifts are critical to zoos advancing their missions, especially in times of shrinking financial support. On the other hand, the sale of these items is far outside the comfort zone of most zoo managers.

For the first twenty years, Riverbanks operated its own modest food stands and gift shops. As the zoo grew in size and scope, so did the demand for improved quality and guest service, and it became evident that managing these facilities was becoming more and more of a distraction. This changed in 1994, when Riverbanks signed a contract with Ogden Entertainment Services, a multinational food and beverage consulting firm, to operate the zoo's retail outlets. In March 2000 the Ogden contract was bought out by ARAMARK, a worldwide food-services manager for cultural attractions, universities, schools, stadiums, and arenas.

By 2012 Riverbanks was generating more than $4 million in annual gross sales of food, beverage, catering, and souvenirs. Approximately 25 percent of that total, or about $1 million, was turned over to the zoo in support of its operations.

Over the years Riverbanks has advanced the zoo's facility rental and catering line of business. Weddings, corporate outings,

(top) The first Kenya Café, pictured here, was owned and operated by Riverbanks Zoo. (bottom) In addition to the traditional stand-alone gift shops, retail carts are strategically located throughout the zoo on busy days.

The Saluda River flows with beauty and history. Pictured here are the remains of bridge abutments from the 1800s.

and other private functions now occur almost daily throughout the zoo and garden grounds. As a result of these activities, a corporate chef, a sous chef, a catering manager, and a banquet captain also joined the Riverbanks team. In 2013 Riverbanks entered into a new food and retail contract with Service Systems Associates of Denver, Colorado.

Stretching across the River

In the years following the zoo's opening, residents on both sides of the river were so pleased with their new zoo that the idea of developing the Lexington property no longer seemed important. This changed in the mid-1980s, when the commission began to discuss the Zoo II expansion plans with members of both county councils. The commission found a receptive audience in the two councils, but several members of Lexington County Council balked, questioning the funding of an expansion plan that again excluded development in their county. After months of discussions, the new $6.35

million bond issue for Zoo II was approved, but with a very clear understanding that any future expansion would have to include a major Lexington County component.

The commission and staff were aware that within a few years the bonds that funded the original zoo would be paid off. This meant that if the two county councils agreed, new bonds could be issued against the existing millage with little or no tax increase. Further analysis indicated that issuing bonds against the existing millage could produce as much as $7 million dollars. The only question was: What can we build on the Lexington County property?

With scenic river views and spectacular valley overlooks, the property was located on the west bank of the Saluda River across from Riverbanks Zoo. In addition to its natural beauty, the site held significant historical value as the location of one of South Carolina's first water-powered textile mills. In addition it was on this spot that General Sherman's troops camped and fired cannons on Columbia prior to marching in and burning the city during the Civil War.

The zoo staff began by developing a list of issues specific to the site. Foremost among these was the incredibly steep, rocky hillside. There was just no way that animal exhibits could be constructed on such a challenging piece of property. Further,

Construction of the bridge that would ultimately connect the zoo and garden.

Did You Know?

Riverbanks horticulturists grow and maintain more than 4,300 species of native and exotic plants—yielding a remarkable 185,000 individual annuals, perennials, ornamentals, woody shrubs, and more.

studies indicated that the hillside soil was quite unstable. This meant that development of the site would have to occur at the top of the hill, a 100-foot rise above the river.

Coincidentally during this time a real estate investor approached Riverbanks about a seventeen-acre parcel of land that

(top) Satch Krantz and Jim Martin, director of horticulture, review plans during construction of the Botanical Garden. The steel supports of the Visitors Center appear in the background. (bottom) Aerial photo of the Botanical Garden.

he owned immediately adjacent to the commission's Lexington property. He was interested in selling the land and wanted to know if the commission would purchase it. The acquisition of this property would prove critical to the future development of the Botanical Garden. Without it the commission would have been forced to build an extremely long and expensive bridge, diagonally across the river, in order to connect the zoo with its Lexington property.

Since a botanical garden had originally been envisioned as a core component of the Riverbanks project, the staff focused its attention on how this might be accomplished. Fortunately this was not as difficult as first imagined.

The zoo had established a very strong horticulture program, developed and managed by then-curator of horticulture Jim Martin. This proved to be quite helpful in that much of the database needed to develop an initial concept already existed in-house.

The commission next employed the talents of one of the nation's leading garden-design firms, Environmental Planning and Design (EPD) of Pittsburgh. EPD partnered with local engineers Wilbur Smith and Associates, whose expertise would be needed in the overall design of the project, including the connector bridge over the Saluda River.

Influential members of the Midlands gardening community also were recruited in order to demonstrate public support. As a result Richland and Lexington County Councils enthusiastically approved a $6 million bond issue for the garden's construction.

Construction began in 1993, and on June 10, 1995, Riverbanks Botanical Garden opened to the public. Just as when the zoo had opened before, visitors were amazed at the facility, from the brick-paved bridge (eight hundred feet long) crossing the Saluda River to the 10,000-square-foot visitors center. The exquisite walled garden showcased intricate detailing along an eight-foot-tall brick wall, a 300-foot-long canal with cascades and pinwheel fountains, and mazes of formal plantings. An antique rose garden was added two years later, featuring 120 varieties of roses including Chinas, teas, and Noisettes. In 2001 the formal entrance opened, complete with a one-mile road from Highway 378, a parking lot, ticket booths, and entry plaza.

In its first fifteen years Riverbanks Botanical Garden (a mere youngster compared to most public gardens) garnered quite a few accolades. In 2004 alone, *Horticulture* magazine named it one of ten gardens that inspire and HGTV placed it among the twenty great public gardens across the United States.

(top) Opening day at Riverbanks Botanical Garden. (bottom) Riverbanks horticulturists routinely maintain five hundred container plantings throughout the zoo and garden. Each pot is changed out twice a year.

Did You Know?

The Botanical Garden has one of the world's largest public collections of Noisettes, known for their sweet perfume, long blooming season, and historical origins in South Carolina. Antique roses have a special connection to South Carolina's culture. The Noisettes were the first class of "old roses" bred, evaluated, and introduced to the world by the United States.

The Old Rose Garden in bloom.

Much of the success of the garden can be attributed to the staff horticulturists, who are exceptionally diligent, talented, and creative. They strive to showcase the best of what nature offers using the latest gardening trends—and prefer to set trends whenever possible. For instance Jenks Farmer, the first (and aptly named) curator of horticulture in the Botanical Garden, pioneered the now-popular concept of planting ornamental kales, cabbages, and mustards as an alternative to the traditional annuals.

The beauty of Riverbanks Botanical Garden lies primarily in its dynamic nature. It is a delightfully orchestrated masterpiece of colors, shapes, textures, and scents. And the landscape continually evolves as plants grow and change. Whether you visited five months ago or five years ago, the garden's "face" changes with the seasons and with the times.

The Science of Plant Keeping

Most people visiting Riverbanks have no idea that the plants are as closely documented as the animals. Staff horticulturists maintain a database that describes all aspects of the Riverbanks plant collection. From the moment a plant arrives, facts are recorded about its size, intended use, origin, and more. Details are also kept on

Blush Noisette Rose—*Rosa* 'Blush Noisette'

COLOR: White flowers

BLOOMING PERIOD: Spring-Fall

TYPE: Shrub

SIZE: 8 feet tall, with pruning
 can be maintained at 4–6 feet

EXPOSURE: Full sun

Old Roses are popular at Riverbanks. One of the staff favorites is
'Blush Noisette,' a tidy rose that fits
nicely into nearly any landscape.
The rose collection at Riverbanks
has never been sprayed with pes-

*'Blush Noisette' was first bred near Charleston, South
Carolina, in 1825 by Phillipe Noisette.*

ticides or chemicals. Many modern roses have lost disease resistance and fragrance
as they have been bred for other traits, but the deliciously, fragrant flowers of 'Blush
Noisette' evoke memories of how roses are really supposed to smell.

the thousands of plants propagated on-site
at Riverbanks, including the propagation
method, location of the parent plant, start
and finish dates, and success rates. Once the
plants are planted, data tracking continues.
Both the zoo and garden are mapped with
designated bed codes that allow staff to
track the location of each and every plant
as well as other details such as date planted,
any insect or disease problems that may

occur, cultural care, flowering and fruiting
times, and even visitor comments. More spe-
cifics are compiled about the native habitat
of each plant, zonal information including heat and cold tolerance, common plant
names, and special care instructions. This
all-encompassing database also contains
digital images of plants in various stages,
information on various plant and bulb sales,
and growth rates and evaluation notes taken

Riverbanks Botanical Garden today boasts seventy acres of natural woodlands, themed gardens and historic ruins. Photograph by Andy Cabe.

by horticulture staff. In a nutshell, the system serves as a giant electronic notebook with plant particulars that have been learned everywhere, from books to the Internet and especially from experience.

Riverbanks Botanical Garden:
Always Something Growing On

To kick off spring each year, thousands of winter-weary garden enthusiasts visit Riverbanks Botanical Garden for Springtime at the Garden, one of the Midlands' premiere gardening festivals. For this one Saturday the garden is transformed into a shopping, educational, and entertainment hub for gardening experts and novices alike. With live music in the amphitheatre and activities for children, this fun family event allows folks of all ages the opportunity to witness the garden at one of its peak times. Thousands of daffodils and tulips and countless other plants in full bloom create a picturesque backdrop for this popular celebration. In addition the Botanical Garden maintains one of the largest public collections of crinum lilies in the United States, with more than one hundred different species and hybrids on display.

The Botanical Garden also opens its back doors one Saturday each spring for its yearly plant sale. What started out as a simple way to offer some of Riverbanks' favorite plants to the public has turned into somewhat of a local phenomenon.

A core group of regular customers shows up hours before the sale opens just to be first in line. Hundreds of others swarm the sale promptly at 9:00 A.M., when the gates open, loading their crates, wagons, and arms with plants. Typically, by 10:00 A.M., half of all the plants are sold—and by the time the sale ends at noon, there are usually just a few hundred remaining out of the nearly five thousand plants originally offered. The sale is Riverbanks' way of offering the public some of the great plants that are grown in the garden, many of which are not available at local retail establishments.

In addition to hosting special events, the garden offers an array of hands-on classes and workshops for all ages through-out the year. One of the highlights is the Junior Master Gardener program, which since 2004 has provided kids ages eight to thirteen the opportunity to get their hands dirty while fostering an appreciation of nature. From propagation to composting, harvesting to weeding, participants "dig in" to real-world gardening through hands-on experiences that teach them how to design, plant and maintain a garden—the backdrop: a one-acre plot of land behind the walled garden. Nature walks through the woods serve as an additional living

(top) A budding gardener participates in one of the Botanical Garden's hands-on workshops. (bottom) One of Riverbanks horticulturists' favorite species tulips, Tulipa clusiana *var.* chrysantha *is smaller than its hybrid cousins but makes up for its size by flowering profusely and consistently. Photograph by Larry Cameron.*

Crinum lily—*Crinum* 'Ellen Bosanquet'

COLOR: Dark pink flowers
BLOOMING PERIOD: Summer
TYPE: Perennial bulb
SIZE: 2 to 3 feet
EXPOSURE: Full sun

Crinum lilies are a huge part of the plant collections at Riverbanks. While there are many great crinums that would work well in the garden, 'Ellen Bosanquet' has been a staple for many years. In mid-summer flower stalks begin to emerge, holding multiple dark-pink, trumpet-shaped flowers.

While most of the crinums grown at Riverbanks are cold hardy, the more tender varieties are also on display in containers during the summer. Photograph by Andy Cabe.

Crinum bulbs are the epitome of durable, persistent bulbs. They can survive long periods of drought and not skip a beat. A mature crinum lily bulb can grow larger than a bowling pin!

classroom to study birds, bugs, and native plants. Junior Master Gardeners follow a detailed curriculum and become certified after successful completion of seven courses.

A Walk through History

Visitors to Riverbanks are often surprised to learn that the site is listed on the National Register of Historic Places. In a futile attempt to prevent General William T. Sherman's army from entering Columbia, in February 1865 Confederate troops burned down the old State Road Bridge, a covered bridge crossing the Saluda River. Sherman countered the effort by immediately ordering the construction of a temporary floating bridge. It is believed that this pontoon may have been made out of

Wild about Riverbanks

. . . when you, years ago, announced the bridge across the Saluda and offered members a chance to purchase bricks with names on them, I made the zoo "ours" by having the name of two of our grandchildren . . . "stamped" on the bridge walk. Since then, our first place [to stop] on every visit is to find the bricks.

This year I added a special memory [on] Feb 17. Nat McCartha and I visited your wonderful improved walking trail to the garden. We stopped on a bench facing the river and the factory and read aloud the article by Dean Hunt in *The Carolina Herald and Newsletter* Oct/Dec 2010 called *The Battle of Beard's Falls* about the military operations around the Saluda Factory Feb 16, 1865. In that beautiful, peaceful setting, we could almost hear the guns.

I realize I haven't mentioned the animals, but the zoo means different things to different people.

Lynn Morris, Little Mountain, S.C.

lumber from the Saluda River Factory, originally located on the Riverbanks site.

Today Riverbanks' visitors can see the vestiges of the covered bridge just east of the Saluda River footbridge connecting the zoo and garden properties. Onlookers walking across can view the original, large granite abutments on opposite banks as well as the supporting pier foundations at the base of two small islands.

The river trail of Riverbanks Garden leads pedestrians from the Saluda River Bridge along a paved path to the ruins of the old Saluda River Factory. One of

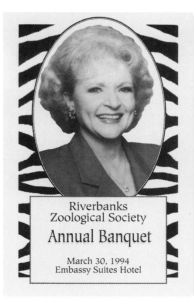

Riverbanks Zoological Society
Annual Banquet
March 30, 1994
Embassy Suites Hotel

Zoo lover Betty White appeared as guest speaker at the Riverbanks Society banquet in 1994. The annual events were later discontinued because of low attendance.

South Carolina's oldest textile mills, the building was constructed out of granite blocks sometime around 1830, and it ultimately became one of the largest cotton mills in the South. At one point the company that owned the factory utilized sixty-four slaves to help operate the mill. Several other businesses were located nearby including a general store, gristmill, tavern and several boarding houses. This area makes up the Saluda Factory Historic District.

The Saluda River Factory struggled financially throughout its history and was sold several times. This misfortune continued when Union troops set it ablaze during Sherman's occupation of Columbia. On the eve of the burning of Columbia, Sherman and his troops set up camp on a ridge just above the factory. From there, on February 17, 1865, they began their assault on the city. A huge boulder known as Sherman's Rock is still visible today along the garden's nature trail.

Following the Civil War the mill was reconstructed, only this time a wood-frame structure was built on the original granite

(top) One of the more interesting features of the old Saluda Factory is this keystone arch that still remains. (bottom) Zoo maintenance staff built the Saluda Mill Interpretive Center from a log-home kit that was donated by Columbia's Southland Log Homes.

Saluda Factory Struggles

The General Assembly chartered the Saluda Manufacturing Company in 1834, and it was one of the first textile factories in the state. The original owners were a group of twelve men led by Davis Ewart. Two undershot wheels, each eighteen feet in diameter, powered the mill, as the eighty looms and thousands of spindles were driven by a series of shafts and belts. The workers were mostly slaves.

Financial demands forced the owners to sell the mill in 1839, and it was sold again shortly after that. Then, in 1855, Col. James G. Gibbes bought and renamed it the Columbia Mills, upgraded the machinery, and added a small woolen mill. Gibbes later sold the factory to three North Carolina investors. In 1865 it was burned to the ground, along with much of the rest of Columbia, by Sherman's Union troops. Sherman in fact launched his invasion of Columbia from the Saluda Mill site.

The factory was rebuilt after the war, but it was consumed by fire again in 1884 and never rebuilt. In 1898 the Columbia Water Power Co. bought the mill ruins and the land and then sold them to Columbia Railway, Gas & Electric Company (now SCE&G) in 1911. In 1970 SCE&G agreed to lease its riverfront property to the Riverbanks Park Commission for one dollar per year for ninety-nine years, and four years later Riverbanks Zoo opened its gates.

Did You Know?

Native flora and fauna flourish along the nature trails at Riverbanks. Year-round the wooded area hosts otters, beavers, muskrats, bobcats, fox, deer, butterflies, and hundreds of species of birds. Nature buffs can also spot mountain laurel, trilliums, and mulberry and pawpaw trees.

Riverbanks' creative horticulturists crafted this beautiful sign out of blocks from the old Central Correctional Institute near Huger Street. The waterfall in the garden's Bog Plaza is also made from these. Photograph by Richard W. Rokes.

foundation. A fire destroyed the mill for a second and final time on the afternoon of August 2, 1884.

From the paved path and covered pavilion along the river trail, Riverbanks visitors can still see remnants of the granite foundations of the mill, picking house, and millrace. One of the more striking features of the mill ruins is a keystone arch immediately adjacent to the path. Careful observers may also notice drill marks on many of the boulders that litter the hillside. These indentations

are the result of a drilling process that split apart the huge rocks in order to produce the blocks of granite used in building the original mill.

Guests can learn even more about the historic site inside the Saluda Factory Interpretive Center, which opened at Riverbanks in April 1999. Featuring drawings and artifacts found on the site, the log cabin at the center of the river trail encourages visitors to learn about the old mill ruins and the history of the land around it.

(above) Pitcher plants in the Botanical Garden's Bog Garden. Photograph by Andy Cabe.
(overleaf) Siamang. Photograph by Richard W. Rokes.

Chapter 4

ANIMAL CARE AND CONSERVATION

Zoo animal medicine was still in its infancy when Riverbanks opened in 1974. At the time most zoos did not employ a full-time veterinarian, relying instead on one or more consulting veterinarians. These were mostly local veterinarians who lacked any kind of formal exotic animal medical training (there basically was no such program available at the time), but they were interested in the unique challenges presented by caring for wild animals.

The zoo's original "hospital" was located in the rear of the administration building. It consisted of a large open area that served as the examination and treatment room, a twelve-foot-square surgery and a small six-foot-square room that doubled as both the laboratory and darkroom for developing X-ray film. Once a week Dr. Russell Van de Grift, a Columbia-based small animal practitioner, would visit the site to conduct rounds, provide whatever treatment was necessary, and on some occasions perform surgery. Van de Grift's orders were carried out over the next six days by a veterinary technician, Satch Krantz.

Although the zoo would later employ two full-time veterinarians, the hospital remained unchanged for the next twenty years. During this time the science of exotic animal medicine advanced tremendously, with a number of veterinary schools offering specialty training in zoo and wildlife medicine. In addition suppliers began to develop and offer a range

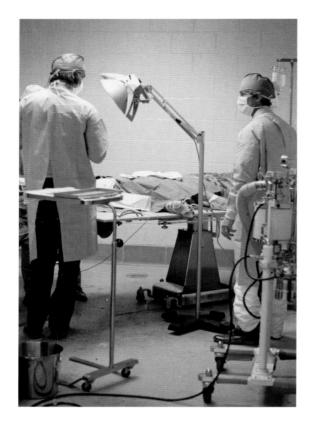

Now president and CEO of Riverbanks, Satch Krantz (left), the zoo's first veterinary technician, is seen here assisting the first veterinarian, Dr. Russell Van de Grift (right).

of specialized equipment and drugs to assist in the growing discipline. However, with limited physical resources, the Riverbanks animal-care staff often became frustrated over the inability to utilize all that was needed in order to maintain optimum health and welfare.

This changed in 1994 with the opening of the new 12,000-square-foot Animal Health and Science Center. As a result the zoo's veterinary hospital grew tenfold overnight. The center includes showers for surgical prep, a state-of-the-art surgical suite, a treatment room, a dedicated X-ray room, and a professional laboratory. It also houses separate, specialized wards for holding animals under treatment and separate spaces for quarantine and necropsy (animal autopsy). The addition of the hospital has made it possible for Riverbanks to provide its animal collection with exemplary medical care and improved quality of life.

Did You Know?

Riverbanks Zoo and Garden is dedicated to providing the highest standards of care to the animals. In 2010 the zoo's veterinary staff, consisting of two veterinarians, two vet technicians, two keepers, one registrar, and two volunteers administered 125 vaccinations, 500 physical exams, and 350 blood draws.

Feeding the Animals

Riverbanks' animals eat a ton! Each year Riverbanks Zoo spends a half million dollars on groceries for the animals. The most expensive animals to feed are the koalas because they only eat certain varieties of eucalyptus leaves—a plant that's hard to come by in South Carolina.

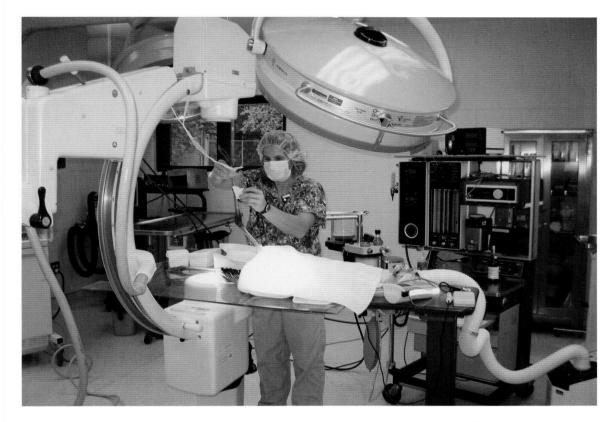

Vet tech Jeanna Lineberger assists with surgery on a young flamingo. The large circular flouroscopy unit allows vets to take real time X-rays during procedures.

Six commissary technicians rotating schedules 365 days of the year work diligently to prepare nearly 300 different diets (or meals) for the animals. Some diets feed one specific animal, and others feed a group. The staff cuts, weighs, measures, and portions out 1,500 ingredients each day to ensure all the animals receive balanced diets.

Just a few of the items included on one year's grocery list are 97,000 pounds of fresh local produce; 38,000 feeder rodents; 787,000 mealworms, waxworms, and fly larvae; 1.4 million crickets; 872 gallons of whole milk (to feed a baby giraffe); 17,080 pounds of eucalyptus; 17,270 pounds of meat, and 125 tons of hay.

My first encounter with Riverbanks was in 1977 as an undergraduate attending professor broke his leg and instead he took us to Riverbanks Zoo. I can remember then thinking to myself, this would be where I would want to work if I ever get into veterinary school as I was absolutely overwhelmed. I cannot even remember how many pictures I took with my little Kodak camera but thus began my lifelong love for the zoo.

As a junior veterinary student in 1981 at the University of Georgia, the American Association of Zoo Veterinarians had a student chapter of which I was a member. We went on a field trip to Riverbanks and during the trip I learned that month-long externships were available to senior veterinary students and upon my return I immediately applied. (I still have my acceptance letter saved amongst my files). I started the externship in the summer of 1982 and during that month was introduced to parrots and many other avian species for the first time not to mention all the other residents of the zoo. This started my career-long love and passion for birds. I remember seeing a juvenile stark-naked Military Macaw that was being hand fed and thought to myself how could something that looked so much like a chicken at the grocery store turn into one of the most magnificent creatures I had ever seen, but he did. I watched him grow and feather out every day that I was there.

I also learned how fragile life could be as we had a juvenile golden lion tamarin that had been born as a twin but the mother rejected him. We kept him in an incubator, providing round the clock feedings. He seemed to be doing so well and thriving but then he suddenly died, thus was my first experience caring for something so young and small only to have it taken away. I made many friends amongst the keepers, curators, and other staff and on subsequent trips have made a point to visit any of them that were on the grounds at the time of my visit. Bob has retired and over the years, I have lost contact with the keepers but the memories of that externship will always be with me. I attribute Riverbanks directly for igniting a spark in me for these animals that I had always been fascinated with but never dreamed I would have the opportunity to work with much less be a part of their care. I was also fortunate to be accepted that same year for a two-month externship at the St. Louis Zoo and the experiences and knowledge I gained at Riverbanks definitely gave me an advantage.

One of my classmates, Dr. Lucy Bartlett, also did an externship at Riverbanks but at a different time. She and I have been planning for years that once her daughter is settled into college, we are going to take one of the safaris led by Satch. Again, a lifelong dream of going to Africa and seeing these animals on their terms and not ours. Dreams do become reality and she and I will take that trip in the near future. My way of giving back to the zoo is by supporting various fund raising events such as the bricks for the snake walk and donating books to the veterinary and general libraries in honor of my parents.

However, these donations will never compare to what Riverbanks gave me.

Dr. Melissa A. Kling, Macon, Ga.

(facing) Golden lion tamarin. Photograph by Richard W. Rokes.

DIET CARD	UPDATED ON: 10/26/2007		COMMON NAME: GORILLA, MALE, MIKE	126
SPECIAL INSTRUCTIONS:			**DIET DELIVERED TO:**	
PM DIET *PM DIET ONLY* NO INGREDIENT OR QUANTITY SUBSTITUTES			RCO	

MONDAY	TUES, SATURDAY	WEDNESDAY
200 GRAMS APPLES	200 GRAMS BANANAS	200 GRAMS APPLES
600 GRAMS CARROTS	600 GRAMS CARROTS	1300 GRAMS CELERY
700 GRAMS CELERY	600 GRAMS CELERY	200 GRAMS ORANGES
200 GRAMS ORANGES	200 GRAMS ORANGES	600 GRAMS SWEET POTATOES

THUR, FRIDAY	SUNDAY
200 GRAMS APPLES	200 GRAMS APPLES
700 GRAMS CELERY	600 GRAMS CARROTS
200 GRAMS ORANGES	600 GRAMS CELERY
600 GRAMS SWEET POTATO	200 GRAMS ORANGES

(top) In the summer of 2008, zoo guests could watch the staff hand-feed five lion cubs through the window of the Bird Conservation Center. (bottom) Diet cards similar to the one shown here are used by commissary techs as a guideline in preparing food for the animals. This card shows just a portion of the afternoon diet of one of the zoo's gorillas.

Scientifically precise animal diets are established by zoo veterinarians with the help of special dietary management software. Commissary technicians refer to diet cards as a tool to help prepare and deliver food to the animals. Each card may only reflect a portion of an animal's diet, since in many cases keepers are responsible for distribution of additional food items that might not necessarily be prepared in the commissary, such as hay, biscuits, or supplements.

It is for this reason that Riverbanks prevents guests from bringing food onto the grounds. Imagine the impact on the animals' nutritional health if thousands of well-intentioned guests bombarded the exhibits with bags of potato chips and peanut butter and jelly sandwiches.

While the role of the zoo's commissary has essentially remained the same over the years, developments in animal science and technology have helped refine the practice. The result: healthier diets and more efficient operations.

Rehabilitating Wildlife

If you ever found an abandoned squirrel in your backyard, you probably needed someone to advise you on how to care for it or even take it off your hands. For years Riverbanks Zoo was the logical resource for people throughout central South Carolina.

Every day people arrive at the zoo's service gate in a virtual parade, usually bearing cardboard boxes or pillow cases. The boxes may contain anything from an abandoned nest of chimney swifts to an injured bald eagle; the pillow cases, any number of snakes or turtles.

The zoo accepted these animals for many years, with little regard to the time, effort or cost involved. Ultimately this got out of hand as abandoned and injured native wildlife filled every nook and cranny of the zoo's buildings. What was worse, on some days the keepers had trouble taking care of the zoo's animals because so much of their day was spent feeding baby squirrels and robins. It was clear something had to be done.

Representatives of various animal welfare organizations were invited to the zoo to discuss the matter. Subsequently the Wildlife Coalition of the Midlands was formed. The coalition was assisted by dedicated volunteers who agreed to take the animals home and care for them, thus relieving the zoo of the burden. The Wildlife Coalition of the Midlands would ultimately cease operations with the success of Carolina Wildlife Care.

(top) One of the hundreds of birds of prey treated in the BB&T Raptor Center. (bottom) Houdini the Harris hawk delighted guests with his aerial acrobats during the daily bird show. Photograph by Ron Brasington.

While small furry koalas are some of the most beloved animals at Riverbanks, they sure can cause an uproar when it comes to their dinner. In order to accommodate these picky eaters, Riverbanks Zoo orders and receives eucalyptus year-round from commercial farms in Arizona and Florida that specialize in growing browse (that is, the fresh, tender vegetation that koalas will eat). Additional eucalyptus is purchased during the warmer months from a farm in Charleston, South Carolina. Other than being expensive (freight charges are a killer), procuring eucalyptus is a rather straightforward process—unless the shipment doesn't arrive. A limited backup supply of browse is kept refrigerated, but it remains palatable to koalas for only a short period of time. So when shipments are late, the staff gets a little concerned.

While Riverbanks has never had a major issue with its browse supply, there have been a few delayed shipments over the years. To help alleviate concerns about delayed eucalyptus shipments, Riverbanks staff built a eucalyptus greenhouse in 2008, solely for growing eucalyptus. The floor of the greenhouse is made up of amended soil so that the eucalyptus trees can be planted directly in the ground, rather than in containers, to produce better browse yields.

Each tree is about four feet tall when planted and given time to grow for a while before the first major pruning occurs. Once established, the trees are pruned to encourage new growth, which is what the koalas eat. Branches must be harvested on a regular basis in order to help maintain height and maximize browse production.

Since the koalas' arrival at Riverbanks in January 2002, the zoo has spent $1.6 million on eucalyptus—seven times the cost of feeding all of the carnivores at the zoo! Photography by Larry Cameron.

Since eucalytpus grows so rapidly, Riverbanks has been able to harvest browse to feed the koalas numerous times throughout the year, while still maintaining a healthy emergency supply. Whenever there is a significant quantity of browse harvested, a portion of a shipment is canceled. With a permanent backup supply firmly in place, Riverbanks' staff can rest a bit easier if a regularly scheduled browse shipment is delayed—and can cut back on a shipment or two, saving the zoo a bit of money and providing the koalas with something they can really sink their teeth into, willingly.

From Andy Cabe, "Growing the Next Koala Café," *Riverbanks*, July/August 2009, p.19.

A peek inside the eucalyptus greenhouse at Riverbanks.

Animal Science

On a daily basis, keepers carefully observe their animals and report on everything from births, weights, and behaviors to diets, physical conditions, and medical concerns. All the information is entered into a real-time, web-based, global database called ZIMS (Zoological Information Management System), which is developed and managed by ISIS (International Species Information System). ISIS is an international, nonprofit organization that collects data from almost eight hundred zoos, aquariums, and related organizations spanning eighty countries. The details entered into ZIMS create a life history of the animals and allows for the collection, reporting, and analyzing of data about both individual animals and groups of animals. In addition the database provides basic biological information on the 2.6 million past and present animals in the collections of the other ISIS members. This vital information helps the animal staff in the daily care and management of the animals in the zoo's collection and allows them to participate in the management of zoo and aquarium animals on a regional and international level.

But the story doesn't end there. In 1996 BB&T made a generous donation that allowed Riverbanks to construct a veterinary medical clinic designed specifically for the treatment of injured raptors (birds of prey) and native endangered species. As a result the Riverbanks Zoo hospital staff has been treating raptors and endangered species for more than twenty-five years. In total more than 3,000 raptors have been assisted. Approximately 150 animals are treated in the Raptor Clinic each year.

Today the BB&T Clinic for Raptors and Endangered Species is financed entirely by private donations and in-kind gifts of medical supplies, pharmaceuticals, and food that these special patients require. The zoo absorbs all other costs.

The clinic has provisions for managing critically ill patients, including hospitalization, radiography, surgery, laboratory support, a pharmacy, and an outside holding areas. Patients are treated on a case-by-case basis and arrive with problems such as gunshot wounds and vehicular collisions. Once stable and eating well, patients take the next step toward eventual release through discharge to the care of a licensed raptor rehabilitator. The birds are then evaluated for their ability to survive in the wild and subsequently prepared for release, a process that can take from several weeks to several months.

Achieving Professional Standards

Riverbanks Zoo and Garden is one of more than 220 zoos and aquariums nationwide

accredited by the Association of Zoos and Aquariums (AZA). Every five years the zoo undergoes a mandatory AZA accreditation process that is designed to ensure that each member institution meets rigorous professional standards for animal welfare, veterinary care, wildlife conservation, scientific research, education, expert staffing, and safety. Last accredited in 2010, Riverbanks is preparing now for its seventh accreditation in 2015.

Fulfilling Our Mission through Conservation

Twenty years ago AZA established the Species Survival Plan (SSP), a long-term effort involving conservation breeding, habitat preservation, public education, field conservation, and supportive research to ensure survival for many of the planet's threatened and endangered species. Currently AZA members are involved in SSP programs for nearly three hundred species. Riverbanks

(left) Ring-tailed lemurs. This baby lemur was born at Riverbanks on April 12, 2004. Photograph by Larry Cameron. (right) Highly endangered golden-headed lion tamarins. Photograph by Richard W. Rokes.

If you haven't been to a zoo in a while, you may have missed something important. Accredited zoos not only have transformed themselves into modern recreational facilities engaged in wildlife conservation projects, but they also have become places where you can learn about and connect to conservation issues important to your community. Every year 175 million people visit AZA-accredited zoos and aquariums, making them vital economic engines as well. The people of Columbia can be proud that Riverbanks Zoo and Garden is a leader in both efforts.

Riverbanks recently achieved a major milestone, receiving its status as an accredited zoo for the sixth time. This twenty-five-year record of meeting the mandatory accreditation standards of the AZA is important because it assures people that they are visiting a zoo that meets or exceeds professional standards.

Fewer than 10 percent of the approximately twenty-four hundred animal exhibitors licensed by the United States Department of Agriculture are AZA accredited. This past summer, the AZA accreditation inspection team observed all aspects of Riverbanks' operations in animal care, keeper training, safety (for animals, staff, and visitors), educational programs, conservation efforts, veterinary programs, financial stability, risk management, and visitor services. Following the rigorous inspection and review by the Accreditation Commission, Riverbanks received the publicly recognized badge that signifies excellence in, and commitment to, animal care, conservation, and education.

The connection to conservation is perhaps the most meaningful aspect of AZA accreditation for the Midlands. AZA's Species Survival Plans manage conservation efforts for more than 300 species of mammals, birds, reptiles, amphibians, fish, and invertebrates. The zoo's participation in these programs links it to an AZA effort that, over the last five years, has supported 2,328 conservation projects in more than 130 countries around the world.

Riverbanks' status as a powerful contributor to the Midlands' economic well-being is equally as impressive. Last year, more than one million people visited the zoo and garden, making it South Carolina's largest tourist attraction. It's important to note that more than 40 percent of these guests originated from beyond a fifty-mile radius around Columbia and, when surveyed, indicated that their sole reason for travel was to visit Riverbanks. A 2008 study by the University of South Carolina placed the overall economic impact of tourists who visit Riverbanks at $60 million a year. Additionally, seven hundred people in the Midlands are employed as a result of Riverbanks' existence. Even despite recent economic challenges, Riverbanks remains a strong and vibrant economic force.

Finally, as environmental and conservation issues become more important to us, having a trusted resource for information and a place for children and families to learn about these critical subjects also becomes more important. South Carolinians can be proud of Riverbanks Zoo and Garden for its commitment to the highest standards of animal care, its contribution to wildlife conservation—locally, regionally, and around the globe—and its service as an educational resource for the community.

From Jim Maddy, president and CEO of the Association of Zoos and Aquariums, "Riverbanks Zoo and Garden: Your Link to Conservation," *Riverbanks,* January/February 2011, p. 9.

participates actively in more than seventy
SSP programs and serves as the leader for
the African lion, Nile hippo, Toco toucan,
Henkel's leaf-tailed gecko, giant leaf-tailed
gecko, mossy leaf-tailed gecko, and satanic
leaf-tailed gecko SSPs. The zoo also sponsors
and maintains studbooks (detailed records

that trace the history of individual species in
zoos) for the fishing cat, false gharial, lined
leaf-tail gecko, spear-point leaf-tailed gecko,
spiny leaf-tailed gecko and Pan's box turtle.
It is difficult to quantify the amount of work
that the dedicated Riverbanks staff com-
mits to the management and conservation

African lion (Zuri).
Photograph by Lynn
Hunter Hackett.

(top) A Sumatran elephant Conservation Response Unit taking down a hut being built by squatters or poachers in Bengkulu Province, Sumatra. (bottom) Sumatran elephant Conservation Response Unit team on patrol.

of these invaluable and sometimes irreplaceable animal populations. However, to provide some perspective, in 2012 Riverbanks' assistant curator of mammals, Sue Pfaff, received AZA honors for *twenty years* of service as the "African Lion Studbook Keeper," an exceptional commitment to a most magnificent species.

In 1996 Riverbanks Society's board of directors established the Riverbanks Conservation Support Fund to provide assistance to local, regional and global conservation initiatives. A total of $87,261 in grants was distributed during fiscal year 2011–12, bringing the total amount provided by the Riverbanks Conservation Support Fund to $417,660 since its inception. Funds have been distributed to 125 different projects in 35 countries around the globe. A few of the projects supported by the fund follow.

SUMATRAN ELEPHANT CONSERVATION RESPONSE UNITS IN BENGKULU PROVINCE, SUMATRA. This conservation effort involves the training of captive elephants for forest patrol. These elephants carry their mahout (elephant trainers) and armed forest rangers to fight forest crime, rescue wild animals, herd wild elephants away from human settlements and fields, and provide community outreach. Project leaders maintain records

Apes are among the mostly highly intelligent and socially complex animals on the planet. Sadly the future for apes in the wild is grim. Ape populations are in rapid decline around the globe, and it is feared that some species may be extinct in the next twenty years. A few years ago, the Association of Zoos and Aquariums (AZA) and its accredited institutions stepped up boldly in a major effort to stem these ape population declines and ensure the long-term survival of such awe-inspiring animals.

In 2011 the AZA's Ape Taxon Advisory Group (TAG) launched the Ape TAG Conservation Initiative, supported by nearly forty AZA member zoos. This significant initiative was designed to provide critical funding to eight field conservation programs for apes—one for each of the great ape species and two for siamangs and gibbons. Riverbanks Zoo currently houses two western lowland gorillas and four siamangs. It is our hope to add orangutans to the collection as part of the Destination Riverbanks capital expansion.

Thanks to the Riverbanks Conservation Support Fund made possible by Riverbanks Society, Riverbanks Zoo and Garden made a three-year financial commitment to the Ape TAG Conservation Initiative. All the funds contributed by AZA zoos were matched by the Arcus Foundation, a leading conservation organization, for an impressive $411,250 generated for ape conservation.

Siamangs have been members of the zoo's animal collection since its opening in 1974. Photograph by Richard W. Rokes.

Riverbanks' contribution to the initiative supported three of the eight field conservation projects, specifically relating to the conservation of bonobos, western lowland gorillas, and Sumatran orangutans.

Excerpt from Ed Diebold, "A Great Ape Effort," *Riverbanks,* May/June 2011, p. 21.

population status of critically endangered vultures in Southeast Asia and will provide insight into how vultures move between nesting and feeding sites. Data collected during the project will also prove critical to future captive management programs and for revitalizing the diversity of wild populations. Ultimately the team will develop a noninvasive mark-recapture protocol for rapidly assessing the conservation status of vultures throughout their Old World range.

ECOLOGY AND CONSERVATION OF KING COBRAS IN THE WESTERN GHATS OF INDIA. This first-ever detailed field study of the king cobra (and the first-ever using radiotelemetry) is designed to learn as much as possible about the natural history and basic ecology of wild king cobras, and to use this information to better manage and conserve the species and the habitat on which it depends. Through radiotelemetry and miniature surgically implanted temperature-data loggers, researchers are examining the species' thermal ecology and activity and have already documented an array of behaviors including male-to-male combat, mate guarding, courtship, mating, predation, and two instances of cannibalism. The project also provides an opportunity to educate Indian students about how to conduct scientific research, including project design and coordination,

Rom Whitaker, director of the Agumbe Rainforest Research Station in Tamil Nadu, India, and his research team radio-tracking a king cobra.

of wild elephant sightings in order to assess the elephant population, control illegal logging, control land encroachment by illegal settlers, and help mitigate human-elephant conflict in the area.

NEW SCIENTIFIC METHODS FOR OLD WORLD RAPTORS. This research combines genetics and field work to assess the

A full-grown Galapagos tortoise.

STATUS—Vulnerable

WHERE IN THE WORLD—Galapagos tortoises are native to the Galapagos Archipelago in the Pacific Ocean west of Ecuador. Riverbanks' "Galaps" are from the island of Santa Cruz. The Galapagos tortoise exhibit was designed with a steep incline so that the tortoises would climb, helping to keep them in good physical condition.

ON THE MENU—In the wild, Galapagos tortoises feed on a wide variety of grasses and herbaceous vegetation. Their zoo diet is composed of high-bulk and low-protein food items to simulate their natural diet.

CLAIM TO FAME—Size. Galapagos tortoises are giants. They are the largest land turtles in the world. Males of the Santa Cruz race can weigh as much as 900 pounds. Riverbanks Zoo's largest male weighs in at 650 pounds.

AMAZING ADAPTATION—Galapagos tortoises can go for extended periods of time without food or water. This helped them to survive the lean times of droughts but also made them a perfect source of fresh meat for sailing ships. Many populations were severely depleted by overcollection by whalers and other sailors.

COOL CHARACTERISTICS—Galapagos tortoises love to be scratched by their keepers. They invite a good scratching by rising up on their legs and stretching out their necks—and they will remain in that position as long as someone is willing to keep scratching the soft skin on their upper legs and neck.

RIVERBANKS' ROLE—Riverbanks successfully hatched Galapagos tortoises for the first time in 2011. The males and one of the females came into the United States in 1928, more than 84 years ago. One of those ancient males was the sire of hatchlings, and a first-time dad at well over a century of age at that. The mother is thought to be at least 70 years old. It is believed that these giant tortoises can live for more than 150 years.

KEEPER'S NOTE—Although many people are not comfortable with other reptiles, most of us really like tortoises. This is especially true of the friendly looking giant tortoise, who has a face like ET. The Galapagos tortoise exhibit at Riverbanks was deliberately designed so that zoo visitors can reach over and touch the animals.

A centenarian is a person who lives beyond the age of one hundred years. You need travel no further than the Galapagos tortoise exhibit at Riverbanks to meet an animal centenarian. Both of Riverbanks' male Galapagos tortoises, Abrazzo and Bravo, arrived in the United States as adults in 1928, which places them at more than one hundred years of age.

Incredibly these tortoises can live to be much older . . . perhaps as long as two hundred years. Adding to the wonder inspired by these grand old creatures, consider the fact that one of Riverbanks tortoises, at the age of one hundred years or more, recently sired five offspring! This is a first hatching of Galapagos tortoises at Riverbanks, and it represents a highly significant event for this species that is considered to be endangered in the wild.

From Ed Diebold, "100 Years in the Making," *Riverbanks,* January/February 2012, p. 24.

Two of the baby Galapagos tortoises that hatched at Riverbanks stand near an adult, allowing for a quick size comparison. The hatchlings lived in an indoor exhibit until it was safe to join the grown-ups. Photography by Larry Cameron.

field techniques, and analysis and presentation of results. Eventually the research team hopes to work with local communities and state forestry officials to designate the area as a king cobra preserve.

In the Field

In addition to distributing grants to outside or international researchers, the Riverbanks Conservation Support Fund also supports field conservation initiatives conducted by Riverbanks' many talented and dedicated staff members. Several of the funded initiatives follow.

EASTERN DIAMONDBACK RATTLESNAKE—
A collaborative field research effort with the South Carolina Department of Natural Resources and other researchers, this project is helping to determine the status of the diamondback and how to prevent further population declines.

TRUMPETER SWAN—With this initiative satellite telemetry is helping staff determine the migratory routes of a restored population of trumpeter swans.

FAUNAL SURVEYS OF CONGAREE CREEK HERITAGE PRESERVE AND CONGAREE NATIONAL PARK—This multiyear survey of the diversity of fishes, amphibians, and reptiles takes place in the unique and as yet unsurveyed South Carolina Heritage

(above) Eastern diamondback rattlesnake. Photograph by Lochlan Baskin. (below) Bird keeper Christine Talleda releases a Caribbean flamingo in Mexico following banding and data collection.

Veterinary technician Jeanna Lineberger scans a loggerhead sea turtle for a Passive Integrated Transponder (PIT) tag in Suriname.

Preserve as well as the Congaree National Park.

FLORAL AND FAUNAL SURVEY OF THE RIVERBANKS SITE—Staff members conduct an inventory of plant and animal species on site and monitor their abundance over time.

RARE NATIVE AMPHIBIAN CAPTIVE HUSBANDRY RESEARCH PROJECT—Biologists in the Aquarium-Reptile Complex are developing captive husbandry techniques for endangered amphibian species in the state including broad-striped dwarf sirens, pine barrens trees frogs, and gopher frogs.

IN SITU KOALA HEALTH SCREENING—In this collaboration with the University of Queensland, staff are studying chlamydia as a limiting factor in wild populations of koalas.

CARIBBEAN FLAMINGO FIELDWORK IN MEXICO—Riverbanks staff have worked in the field as a part of the Caribbean Flamingo Wildlife Research since 1999, conducting research to enhance our understanding of the natural history, migration routes, nutrition, and parental care of wild Caribbean flamingos.

SEA TURTLE RESEARCH AND CONSERVATION IN SURINAME—Riverbanks has partnered with the World Wildlife Fund and the Sea Turtle Conservation to conduct research on leatherback and green sea turtles at

Galibi and Matapica beaches in Suriname. During the 2011 and 2012 field seasons, Riverbanks staff partnered to mount twenty-four satellite transmitters on these turtles in an effort to understand better their on-shore movements and long-distance migrations with the goal of applying this knowledge to species conservation.

RING-TAILED LEMUR RESEARCH AND CONSERVATION IN MADAGASCAR—In partnership with the University of Colorado and the University of North Dakota, Riverbanks' veterinary medical staff have worked in the field to conduct a comparison of health parameters of wild ringtailed lemurs across two habitats and with varied levels of human disturbance at the Beza Mahafaly Special Reserve, Madagascar.

Attaining the Highest Honors

At the September 2011 AZA Annual Conference in Atlanta, Riverbanks was honored with a fifth Edward H. Bean Award for its long-time commitment to the endangered Bali Mynah. The Bean Award, established in 1956, is highly sought after and esteemed among North American zoo

Riverbanks Field Conservation

Thanks to the inspiration of Bob Davidson, former president of the Riverbanks Society board of directors, the Riverbanks Field Conservation Associates Program was initiated in 2011. This internal competitive application process allows for Riverbanks staff in all areas to apply to participate in local/regional and international conservation projects. To date, Riverbanks staff members have participated in field conservation projects for Humboldt penguins in Peru; diamondback terrapins, leatherback sea turtles, bog turtles, hellbenders, and indigo snakes in Georgia; gopher tortoises in South Carolina; and leatherback and green sea turtles in Suriname, South America.

professionals. Originally the award was given in recognition for the most significant birth or hatching of a species, but it has since evolved to acknowledge animal-management programs that contribute to the long-term reproductive success of one or more species.*

The following is a summary of Riverbanks' Edward H. Bean Awards and other associated awards for animal conservation and exhibit design. These are truly world-class accomplishments.

*Portions of this section on the Edward H. Bean Awards and others achievements were adapted from Ed Diebold, "Riverbanks Zoo's Award Winning Animal Programs," Riverbanks, January/February 2012, pgs. 3–8.

Hymenocallis coronaria, commonly known as the Rocky Shoals spider lily, is a plant native to Richland and Lancaster Counties in South Carolina. Listed as a plant of national concern, this plant is imperiled statewide in South Carolina and is on Georgia's endangered species list.

For those unfamiliar with the beauty of this rare plant, the spider lily is a bulbous breed related to the amaryllis. Its name, the "Rocky Shoals spider lily," comes from its preferred habitat—rivers in which fast-moving, well-oxygenated water passes over rocks. Such environments are found in the Saluda and the Broad Rivers near the convergence that forms the Congaree River. The rocky shoals found in these locations are prime habitats for *Hymenocallis coronaria.*

Peak flowering usually occurs, and blooms become visible, from mid-May to mid-June here in South Carolina. Intermittent flowering continues throughout the summer. Each plant sends up one to three flower stalks, with as many as six to nine flowers on each stalk. Shortly after flowering, the plant will drop mature seeds into the water. These seeds sink to the bottom of the river or are carried away by currents until they subsequently wedge themselves into a rock crevice or wash onto sandy, rocky riverbanks and begin to grow.

Existing wild spider lily populations are in danger of disappearing. Their beauty attracts collectors and plant enthusiasts. Wild collecting of plants such as these, whose natural range is so localized and sparse, can cause declines in population. Also changes in water flow and water quality can be of utmost concern with any aquatic species. If the water flow increases too much, an entire colony could potentially be destroyed. Too little water flow deprives the flowers

(right, top) Wild populations of spider lilies reside in the Saluda and Broad Rivers. (right, bottom) Members of the Rocky Shoals spider lily preservation team map the locations of wild spider lilies.

of essential seed-carrying capacity. Most often changes in water flow and water quality are caused by transportation along the water way, recreational activities, run-off pollution, or use of the water for generation of electricity and/or drinking water.

There is a growing need for the preservation of spider lilies as a result of the decrease in native populations. For several years now, Riverbanks Zoo and Garden has been collecting seeds in an attempt to find the best means of growing this plant in a nursery setting.

In 2005 a Rocky Shoals spider lily preservation team was assembled consisting of the City of Columbia, South Carolina Electric and Gas Company, River Alliance, South Carolina Department of Natural Resources (SCDNR), U.S. Fish and Wildlife Service (USFWS), and Riverbanks Zoo and Garden. The team's goal is preservation, that is, to reestablish spider lilies in their natural environment along stretches of the Broad, the lower Saluda, and the Congaree Rivers.

The project's genesis was brought about through the relicensing of the Columbia Hydroelectric Project by the Federal Energy Regulatory Commission. The hydroelectric project, currently owned by the City of Columbia and operated by Lockhart Power, is situated on the Broad River near the confluence of the Broad and Saluda Rivers. The River Alliance became involved since the plant is found in many spots where the Three Rivers Greenway is being developed. The SCDNR and the USFWS serve as resource managers providing oversight and guidance for reintroduction of new plants and management of existing colonies.

Currently the Riverbanks staff participates in an annual Rocky Shoals Spider Lily Survey each spring where the existing populations of spider lilies are mapped on GPS. This data, when assimilated over a number of years, will help determine the long-term population growth or decline of *Hymenocallis coronaria*.

Rocky shoals spider lily—Hymenocallis coronaria.

The Riverbanks staff also collects *Hymenocallis coronaria* seeds each summer and brings them back to grow them at our greenhouse facilities. Once these seedlings begin to form bulbs, they are planted in clusters in large tubs. After one to two years, these plants are removed from tubs, and the intermingled masses of roots help to form a mat of sorts. This mat of bulbs is then reintroduced into the river and secured using large river rocks. The mat technique seems to be yielding greater success than previous efforts of planting individual plants back into the river.

Where do we go from here? The involved parties will continue to work on monitoring and reintroducing *Hymenocallis coronaria* back into its native environment in the Broad and Congaree Rivers. These efforts will hopefully ensure that the Rocky Shoals spider lily is enjoyed for generations to come.

From Andy Cabe and James R. Deveraux, "Saving a Spider Lily," *Riverbanks*, July/August 2007, p. 8.

Bali Mynah—*Leucopsar rothschildi*

The critically endangered Bali mynah.

STATUS—Critically endangered

WHERE IN THE WORLD—Bali mynahs live in the Birdhouse at Riverbanks along the Asian Trek. In the wild, they can be found only on the Indonesian island of Bali, where they almost became extinct but are now making a comeback because of the successes of zoo breeding programs.

ON THE MENU—These birds eat a variety of fruits and special bird pellets from which they get all of the important nutrients they need for excellent health. In the wild, Bali mynahs eat small berries, insects, and small amphibians.

CLAIM TO FAME—The Bali mynah is the national bird of Bali.

AMAZING ADAPTATION—Bali mynahs are extremely gregarious and have a good memory. They can even remember where to locate fruiting trees from the previous year.

COOL CHARACTERISTICS—As part of a courtship ritual, the male Bali mynah will throw back its head before delivering a loud, characteristic call.

KEEPER'S NOTE—Bali mynahs are the most inquisitive birds in their exhibit, always waiting near the door for keepers to arrive with their favorite foods: worms and crickets.

2011—BALI MYNAH

The Bali mynah is a critically endangered species that has been maintained and bred at Riverbanks since opening. Then-curator of birds Bob Seibels recognized the key role AZA-accredited institutions could play in saving this enigmatic species. He established both the AZA Bali Mynah Regional Studbook and the Species Survival Plan. Since then Riverbanks has bred forty-five Bali mynahs, and the Bali mynah program has become synonymous with the name

"Riverbanks." The program's success has led to a flourishing zoological population to the extent that the species is no longer on the edge of extinction, as it once was, and may conceivably provide the springboard for future reintroductions back into the wild.

2010—SIGNIFICANT ACHIEVEMENT FOR THE LONG-TERM PROPAGATION AND CONSERVATION PROGRAM FOR BLACK-FOOTED CAT

In 1994 the Riverbanks animal-care team committed themselves to reestablishing the rapidly declining black-footed cat population in North America. Since the program's inception Riverbanks has produced twenty offspring, a significant contribution to the captive population. The timing of Riverbanks' reproductive success with the species coincided with the time of the population's greatest need. Without this contribution at the appropriate time, any likelihood of the North American population achieving self-sustainability would have been lost.

2005—MALAGASY LEAF-TAILED GECKO LONG-TERM PROPAGATION AND CAPTIVE HUSBANDRY PROGRAM

Malagasy leaf-tailed geckos are a group of lizards found exclusively on the island of Madagascar. The translation of the

generic name *Uroplatus* is "flat tail," an apt description of this gecko's long, dorsaventrally flattened tail. These geckos are completely arboreal (that is, they live in trees), exquisitely camouflaged, and quite bizarre-looking animals. They are all dependent on primary forest cover for their survival. Unfortunately the forests in Madagascar are rapidly being destroyed. Riverbanks began working with leaf-tailed geckos almost two decades ago. Much of what is known about the long-term husbandry of leaf-tailed geckos has been discovered at Riverbanks. To date more than one thousand leaf-tailed geckos have

Bob Seibels, Riverbanks' curator of birds, and Kevin Bell, curator of birds at Lincoln Park Zoo in Chicago (now president and CEO), examine Bali mynahs in Indonesia prior to their release back into the wild.

Black-footed cat and kittens. Photograph by Richard W. Rokes.

STATUS—Listed as vulnerable by the International Union for the Conservation of Nature (or IUCN), this solitary and secretive feline often seeks refuge at the slightest disturbance, retreating into old termite mounds or the abandoned burrows of other mammals.

WHERE IN THE WORLD—In the wild, black-footed cats inhabit arid semideserts and savannas of South Africa, Namibia, and Botswana. At the zoo black-footed cats can be found in the Riverbanks Conservation Outpost exhibit.

ON THE MENU—Be careful not to assess this animal's disposition and appetite based on size alone. The black-footed cat is a very skilled and ferocious hunter preying on several small rodents and birds in one night to satisfy its large energy requirements.

CLAIM TO FAME—Tiny but terrifying. This small and shy felid can become fierce when provoked. Legend among native Bushmen claims that the black-footed cat can kill a giraffe by piercing its jugular. Although this is purely legend, it was intended to characterize the persistent and fearsome nature of this little feline.

KEEPER'S NOTE—On July 12, 2012, animal keepers inserted an infrared camera into a tunnel leading to the underground black-footed cat den and discovered two black-footed cat-kittens. The litter size can vary from one to four. The birth of these two increased the number of black-footed cats born at Riverbanks to twenty-two and is quite significant in terms of the captive population.

hatched at Riverbanks and been placed with other AZA institutions, a remarkable long-term commitment to the management and conservation of these species.

1998—Long-term Propagation Program for Ramphastids (Toucans, Toucanettes, and Aracaris)

In 1977 Riverbanks Zoo achieved a world first with the successful fledging of three Toco toucan chicks. At the time it was considered virtually impossible to breed large toucans in captivity. Thanks to the skill and attention to detail demonstrated by the bird department's staff, this would be the first of *many* such successes. Since then more than fifty Toco toucans have been raised to maturity as well as forty-five specimens of five other toucan species. Riverbanks staff created the husbandry manual on toucan care and breeding. The zoo remains actively involved in the SSP. Riverbanks' senior veterinarian also serves as the veterinary adviser for the Taxon Advisory Group that oversees toucan populations in North American zoos.

1982—Black Howler Monkey Propagation

Black howler monkeys were first acquired for the Riverbanks collection in 1974, at a time when the captive husbandry for the species was poorly understood. Zoos maintaining the species faced significant challenges with nutrition and behavior. For a number of years Riverbanks maintained a robust commitment to the species and succeeded in developing husbandry techniques and veterinary protocols to address the species's needs. Many of these techniques and protocols are still in use today.

International Conservation Awards

Conservation is the AZA's top priority. AZA International Conservation Awards are bestowed on institutions that excel in the areas of habitat preservation, species restoration, and overall support of the world's biodiversity. Most recently, in 2012, Riverbanks received an International Conservation Award for its financial support of the Grevy's Zebra Trust (GZT) along with twenty-six other zoo partners. The GZT is a conservation trust based in Kenya. It was established in order to address the urgent need to conserve the declining Grevy's zebra population in the community rangelands of Kenya and Ethiopia. The GZT works with local community conservancies in northern Kenya to develop wildlife and habitat management schemes that favor Grevy's zebras and other wildlife.

In 2003 Riverbanks received an International Conservation Award for the Rodrigues Fruit Bat Conservation Program

Photograph by Sean Foley.

STATUS—Little is known about the status of leaf-tailed geckos in the wild. Unfortunately, what has become quite clear is that their forest habitat is disappearing at an alarming rate. In addition to severe habitat destruction, leaf-tailed geckos are collected for the pet trade, putting further pressure on already stressed populations. Without protection of vital primary rainforests, their future in the wild is murky at best.

WHERE IN THE WORLD—Leaf-tailed geckos occupy a wide variety of habitats on the island of Madagascar. Riverbanks not only displays several different species but also maintains a large off-display colony of leaf-tailed geckos.

ON THE MENU—Insectivores, leaf-tailed geckos will feed on a wide variety of arthropods including moths, crickets, and cockroaches. Crickets make up their main diet at the zoo.

CLAIM TO FAME—Bug-eyed! Leaf-tailed geckos are known for their strange, even bizarre physical appearance. They have seemingly oversized heads and large bulging eyes. Some have tails that look like a rolled-up leaf while others resemble a flying squirrel's tail. They can have horns over their eyes or fringes along their jaws and can be as small as three inches long or more than a foot in length. All possess absolutely perfect camouflage that makes them look more like moss, lichens, and leaves than lizards.

AMAZING ADAPTATION—Leaf-tailed geckos have the ability to adhere to and walk on almost any vertical surface including glass. The bottoms of their toes are covered with lamellae, which in turn bear as many as a million tiny hair-like bristles called setae. Each setae is then split up into thousands of even smaller spatulae that can hold onto any microscopic unevenness in a surface. This gives the gecko the unusual ability to walk upside-down.

COOL CHARACTERISTICS—The giant leaf-tailed gecko is one of the largest geckos in the world and has more marginal teeth than any other reptile, bird, or mammal. Why it has so many teeth is unknown. Fortunately its teeth are very small and its jaws fairly weak, so a bite from one of these geckos won't even break the skin.

RIVERBANKS' ROLE—There are currently fourteen recognized species of leaf-tailed geckos. Of these Riverbanks has managed to successfully reproduce eight different species, hatching more than a thousand eggs. Riverbanks' long-term commitment to reproductive and captive husbandry research for this group of enigmatic lizards led to the prestigious AZA Bean Award in 2005.

KEEPER'S NOTE—Female leaf-tailed geckos have a fondness for escargot. The gastropods are either crushed or swallowed whole. The snails' shells are full of calcium, which is used by the female geckos to produce their eggs. An adult female may consume twenty to thirty land snails a year. A giant leaf-tailed gecko can swallow a snail the size of a quarter.

Toco Toucan—*Ramphastos toco*

The Toco toucan is known for its long, colorful beak.

STATUS—Uncommon

WHERE IN THE WORLD—Toucans live at the zoo in heavily planted enclosures. In the wild they can also be found in dense forests or along the forest's edge.

ON THE MENU—At the zoo Toco toucans eat a variety of fruits and special bird pellets that contain all the important nutrients they need for excellent health.

CLAIM TO FAME—The "Fruit Loops" bird

AMAZING ADAPTATION—The toucan's famously long beak is used to pluck berries from thin branches.

COOL CHARACTERISTICS—Toucans, related to woodpeckers, hang on the sides of trees to hammer out a nest cavity.

KEEPER'S NOTE—Riverbanks has bred more Toco toucans than any other private or public collection in the world. Every year, several chicks hatch at the zoo, and the parents raise the chicks themselves. Keepers provide a lot of live crickets during this time because that is all the chicks will eat until they are about a week old.

along with the Philadelphia Zoo, Oregon Zoo, Disney's Animal Kingdom, Woodland Park Zoo, Roger Williams Park Zoo, Blank Park Zoo, John Ball Zoo, Folsom Children's Zoo, and Biodome de Montreal. This project, carried out in partnership with the AZA Bat Taxon Advisory Group, was responsible for the hiring of a Rodriguan environmental educator who has served to educate, motivate, and coordinate sustainable behavior and positive environmental action for Rodriguans of all ages.

In 2002 Riverbanks received the award for the Tree Kangaroo Conservation Program

A pair of black howler monkeys. Don't let the name fool you—only the males are actually black. Photograph by Larry Cameron.

STATUS—The exact population density of the black howler monkey is not known, and there is some disagreement as to whether it should be classified officially as threatened. Unfortunately howler monkey habitat is being destroyed through deforestation, and the primates are hunted for their meat, so it is vital to protect this species to ensure survival.

WHERE IN THE WORLD—Black howler monkeys are native to Bolivia, Argentina, Paraguay, and Brazil. Be sure to look for them at Riverbanks in the Conservation Outpost.

ON THE MENU—Strict herbivores, black howler monkeys eat only leaves, fruits, and flowers in the wild. At Riverbanks they eat lettuce, vegetables, fruit, and supplements specially formulated for primates. Their favorites include grapes, bananas, and sweet potatoes.

AMAZING ADAPTATION—If you watch a howler monkey, you may notice it swinging by its tail. This prehensile tail can grip branches and support the monkey's full weight—almost like having another hand. The agile tail aids in movement through trees and also keeps the monkey from falling, should it lose its grip.

RIVERBANKS' ROLE—In 1982 Riverbanks received the prestigious Edward H. Bean Award from the Association of Zoos and Aquariums (AZA) for outstanding success with captive breeding of the black howler monkey. Riverbanks continues to participate in this program actively and collaborates with other AZA-accredited zoos to increase the genetic diversity of the species, thus ensuring a healthy, self-sustaining population.

KEEPER'S NOTE—These noisy primates usually howl at dawn and dusk as a means of communication and to locate other howlers. Howler monkeys can be heard for miles through the forests, thanks to an enlarged hyoid bone in the throat that amplifies sound. Their raucous voices may be used to keep a troop together but more often are used to keep separate troops apart. The call of a male is louder and deeper than that of a female so they can easily differentiate between the two. Black howler monkeys also tend to howl when it is raining—and in fact the two animals at Riverbanks howl whenever keepers refill their water bowls with a hose.

along with Roger Williams Park Zoo, Calgary Zoological Society, Columbus Zoo and Aquarium, Gladys Porter Zoo, Kangaroo Conservation Center, Miami Metro Zoo, Milwaukee County Zoo, Oregon Zoo, Philadelphia Zoo, Pittsburgh Zoo and PPG Aquarium, San Antonio Zoo, Santa Fe Community Teaching College, Woodland Park Zoo, and the Zoological Society of San Diego. The Tree Kangaroo Conservation Program is based at Seattle's Woodland Park Zoo, and Riverbanks has adopted a community-based strategy to conserve the species and its native habitat on the Huon Peninsula of Papua New Guinea. The program currently works with local villages and landowners to manage the country's first conservation area, which covers an amazing 187,000 acres of prime habitat in one of the world's most biologically diverse region.

The Riverbanks Conservation Support Fund Review Committee strives to balance its support between international and local/regional conservation initiatives. Between the years of 2007 and the present, nearly ninety thousand dollars have been distributed in support of local/regional conservation efforts. In recognition of this emphasis on the native wildlife and wild places, the South Carolina Wildlife Federation presented Riverbanks with its Wildlife Conservation Award in 2012.

Also in 2012, the South Carolina Department of Health and Environmental Control recognized the Riverbanks comPOOst program with its Earth Day Award. In 2008 Joy Shealy, professional engineer of Shealy Engineering in Irmo, South Carolina, donated her time and expertise to draft a composting-facility management plan for Riverbanks. As a result approximately fifteen thousand cubic feet of animal waste that once went to a landfill is now converted into rich compost for use with plantings at Riverbanks as well as for sale to Riverbanks members and guests. Net revenues from comPOOst sales in turn go into the Conservation Support Fund to support additional conservation efforts.

From start to finish, the Riverbanks comPOOsting process takes about three months. Riverbanks' four African elephants are the main contributors, making up nearly 75 percent of the fifteen hundred pounds of manure added to the pile on a daily basis.

A herd of Grevy's zebras in Northern Kenya. Photograph courtesy of Saint Louis Zoo.

STATUS—Endangered. This species has undergone one of the most substantial range reductions of any African mammal and faces an extremely high risk of extinction in the wild. Overall numbers of Grevy's zebras have declined from an estimated 15,000 in the late 1970s to current estimates of between 2,000 and 2,500.

WHERE IN THE WORLD—Grevy's zebras are found only in northern Kenya and southern Ethiopia.

ON THE MENU—Broad-leaved plants and grasses

CLAIM TO FAME—Size. The largest of all zebras, the Grevy's zebra can easily be identified by its rounded ears and narrow stripes.

COOL CHARACTERISTICS—One hour after birth, a newly born zebra can walk and even run for short distances. Each zebra is born with a unique pattern of stripes, much like human fingerprints. The stripes actually serve as camouflage from predators. When in groups, the zebras' stripes make it difficult for approaching prey to single out its victim.

AMAZING ADAPTATION—Living in mostly arid and semiarid deserts, Grevy's zebras can go without water for up to five days. Today, however, the distances between available food sources and water is greater than ever, which forces the zebras to travel greater lengths. Milk-producing females are particularly affected by this, which can have consequences for the survival of their foals.

KEEPER'S NOTE—While Riverbanks does not house Grevy's zebras, the zoo does have two Grant's zebras.

STATUS—Rodrigues fruit bats are endangered and quite susceptible to drastic changes in their environment. In the late 1960s, the overall population declined as a result of deforestation and extreme weather conditions, specifically cyclones. Today there are perhaps 1,000 Rodrigues fruit bats surviving on Rodrigues Island.

WHERE IN THE WORLD—The Island of Rodrigues (in the Indian Ocean off the coast of Madagascar). At the zoo visitors can see the bats inside the Riverbanks Conservation Outpost.

ON THE MENU—Fruit, pollen, and nectar. Grapes are a favorite of the bats at the zoo. Fruit bats drink water by swooping down on a body of water to gulp a drink on the fly. Some species have even been known to consume seawater, believed to replace mineral salts not obtained from their diet.

CLAIM TO FAME—Flying mammals. While some mammals are capable of gliding, bats are the only mammals capable of true flight.

AMAZING ADAPTATION—The normal resting position for bats is upside-down because their delicate bones are adapted for flight instead of supporting their weight.

COOL CHARACTERISTICS—Unlike what many people believe, fruit bats have excellent eyesight for travel and to locate food. Large fruit bats are often referred to as flying foxes because of their elongated muzzles that give them their foxlike appearance.

Resting upside-down.

KEEPER'S NOTE—Rodrigues fruit bats have a wingspan of 2.5 to 3 feet. Their wings are actually thin skin stretched between the fingers and thumb of each hand. Fruit bats are a highly beneficial species for the environment, serving as pollinators of native plants and dispersing the seeds that they eat.

STATUS—Endangered

WHERE IN THE WORLD—The Matschie's tree kangaroo lives in the mountainous rainforests of northeastern New Guinea. Visitors to Riverbanks can see the tree kangaroo most anytime inside the Riverbanks Conservation Outpost, but they are most active during their feeding times, normally around 10 A.M. and 3 P.M.

ON THE MENU—In the wild, the tree kangaroo usually eats leaves and fruits. At Riverbanks it dines on apples, carrots, sweet potatoes, corn on the cob, green leaf lettuce, high-fiber monkey biscuits, and various types of native browse.

AMAZING ADAPTATION—Tree kangaroos are arboreal animals, meaning they spend most of their time residing in trees rather than on the ground. Their arms and legs are similar lengths, and their strong curved claws help them as they climb trees. Tree kangaroos are known to be clumsy climbers, so their long stiff tail is used to maintain balance as they move from one branch to another.

RIVERBANKS' ROLE—Riverbanks Zoo is committed to helping the endangered tree kangaroo thrive not only through a captive breeding program but also by monetarily supporting the Tree Kangaroo Conservation Program (TKCP) in Papua New Guinea. TKCP promotes wildlife conservation and forest protection through awareness walking tours, as well as through school presentations and informal conservations with landowners. Since tree kangaroo hunting is culturally important to the clan of Papua New Guinea, the TKCP advocates sustainable hunting rather than a complete ban. Education is essential for winning support from landowners to conserve land while increasing local awareness of conservation issues. The research aspect of the TKCP is to collect data to estimate local populations of tree kangaroos, radio collar

Photograph by Larry Cameron.

individual tree kangaroos to determine movement patterns and home ranges, and lastly collect DNA from fecal samples to determine genetic structure of the local population.

KEEPER'S NOTE—Tree kangaroos have lived at Riverbanks since 1974. The staff at Riverbanks has been fortunate that the male, Mambawe, and the female, Patch, choose to live together in the same exhibit. In the wild, male tree kangaroos are solitary, except during breeding season. A strong bond is formed between mother and offspring; Patch has demonstrated this with each of her three joeys: Wantok, Kasbeth, and Kuabe.

Juvenile loggerhead sea turtle. Photograph by Richard W. Rokes.

STATUS—Threatened (under the Endangered Species Act)

WHERE IN THE WORLD—Loggerheads are world travelers; they can be found in tropical and subtropical oceans and coastal areas around the world. This includes the coast of South Carolina. In fact the largest nesting area for loggerheads is in the southeastern United States, from Florida to North Carolina. At Riverbanks Zoo you can find this species on display in the Atlantic Reef tank.

ON THE MENU—The strong jaws of a loggerhead can crush its prey. Loggerheads eat lots of crustaceans (crabs and shrimp), mollusks, and fish, and they especially love a treat of moon jellies from time to time. Aquarists mimic this diet at the zoo by providing lots of different options of seafood, meticulously managing the amount of food fed to the turtle each day in order to ensure a proper growth rate. Turtles love to eat, after all.

CLAIM TO FAME—Loggerheads are known for nesting on South Carolina beaches. Female sea turtles will come to shore during the nesting season (April through September) and lay up to seven nests during this time. Each nest contains an average of 120 eggs, which will incubate under the sand for approximately 55 days. Loggerheads are very well known for their nest hatching behavior, in which all the eggs will hatch at once, and hatchling turtles will climb their way to the surface of the sand. Their emergence is called a "boil" as dozens of turtles seemingly appear out of nowhere and scramble for the sea.

AMAZING ADAPTATION—Sea turtles are marine reptiles, but they breathe air. They can stay submerged for many hours between each breath.

COOL CHARACTERISTICS—Mostly solitary animals, sea turtles only associate for courtship and mating. Females are thought to return to the beach where they were born in order to nest, but males likely spend their entire lives at sea.

RIVERBANKS' ROLE—Since the opening of the ARC in 1989, Riverbanks has displayed sea turtles. Each turtle that lives at Riverbanks is eventually released back into the wild, in cooperation with the South Carolina Department of Natural Resources, and this treatment is much like a "headstart" program. The turtles receive special tags that enable scientists to track the turtles if they are ever encountered by anyone fishing or on a beach in the future, possibly yielding valuable life-history information. Riverbanks has released more than one hundred turtles back into the wild.

KEEPER'S NOTE—These turtles are highly intelligent, so aquarists use special training techniques to help manage the feeding frenzy at meal times on exhibit. Instead of just tossing the food into the tank, aquarists target-feed each turtle to be sure it eats all of his diet, and nothing extra. The process starts when the turtle gets used to seeing a feeding pole, then the turtle is rewarded for coming over to the pole and eventually touching it. Over time the turtle learns that the pole means it's time to come over to the aquarist for food; in this way the tank of fish and the individual turtle can be fed without any conflicts or missed meals.

The gigantic leaves of the upright elephant ear are easily recognizable. Photograph by Andy Cabe.

COLOR: Green leaves
BLOOMING PERIOD: Grown for foliage
TYPE: Tropical perennial
SIZE: 6 feet tall
EXPOSURE: Full sun

The horticulturists at Riverbanks Zoo are always looking for plants that give visitors a tropical feel. *Alocasia macrorrhiza* is a winner all the way around. Its leaves are huge, the bulb multiplies quickly, and it has few pests. This is also one of the few plants at Riverbanks that has turned into a popular photo op for families.

(above) 'Reve d' Or' translates as "dream of gold." A fitting name for this lovely, semi-double-flowered climbing rose, whose yellow-tinged blooms can appear from spring until fall. Photograph by Andy Cabe. (overleaf) Red-ruffed Lemur. Photograph by Richard W. Rokes.

Chapter 5

THE NEW ZOO

In the early 1990s Earl Wells, the late director of the Ft. Wayne Children's Zoo in Ft. Wayne, Indiana, had a wonderfully creative concept. He was looking for a way to generate revenue for his zoo yet wanted to do so in a fun and educational way. Wells believed a traditional wooden carousel would be a big hit with his young guests, but he wanted it to be unique to the zoo. Why not replace the carousel's horses and other historical figures with exotic animals? With nothing more than a vague concept he approached Carousel Works in Mansfield, Ohio, the largest manufacturer of wooden carousels in the world. Their collaboration produced the very first Endangered Species Carousel, which opened in the Ft. Wayne Children's Zoo in 1994.

Three years later Riverbanks became the second zoo to add an Endangered Species Carousel. The decision to bring in a carousel was not made lightly because until then Riverbanks had been, in its purist form, a zoological park. Some feared that, by adding what is essentially a carnival ride, Riverbanks could be taken in a whole new direction. This concern was weighed against the relatively inexpensive cost of the carousel compared to the cost of a major new animal exhibit. Further, as had been the case with the Ft. Wayne Children's Zoo, the commission and staff wanted to provide Riverbanks' guests with a fun, enjoyable experience. The zoo's carousel opened in 1997 and was an instant hit.

Based on the popularity of the Endangered Species Carousel, the staff began to

fun-filled outing for the entire family. Perhaps more important, these activities generate significant revenue that in turn allows the zoo and garden to reinvest in the animals and in guest services while pumping tourist dollars back into the Midlands economy.

Zoo 2002

As the twentieth century came to a close, Riverbanks Zoo was poised to take the next great step in its development as one of America's great zoos. In December 1997 Richland and Lexington County Councils passed the most ambitious bond issue in Riverbanks history—$15 million. This was supplemented by a $4.5 million private capital campaign. Together the bond issue and fund drive marked the single largest capital investment in the zoo's history. Known collectively as Zoo 2002, the funds were used to make a number of improvements to the zoo and garden over a three-year period.

Construction started in 1999 for the $19 million expansion project. A year later, the new entrance plaza and lemur exhibits opened. By 2001 the Botanical Garden entrance opened to the public as well as a number of new bird exhibits, including the 6,000-square-foot Bird Conservation Center, fourteen outdoor aviaries for cold-tolerant species, and the 12,000-square-foot Birdhouse at Riverbanks.

The Endangered Species Carousel has revolved nearly 3 million turns since its opening. Here two children take a spin. Photograph by Robin Vondrak Photography.

consider additional activities that might enhance the guest experience. Armed with studies indicating that zoo visitors are eager to interact with the animals, the zoo next provided an opportunity to feed one of the most charismatic members of the collection, the giraffes.

With the success of the carousel and giraffe feeding, a number of interactive attractions quickly followed. Guests can now climb a rock wall, ride ponies and a children's train, feed lorikeets and navigate a four-story-tall ropes course. Today a visit to Riverbanks is a more dynamic and

The new state-of the-art Birdhouse featured three geographically themed bird habitats: Penguin Coast, a 1,350-square-foot penguin habitat with underwater viewing; Asian Trek, featuring birds such as the giant hornbill and the rare Bali mynah; and Savanna Camp, showcasing the birds of the arid African and South American savannas. Recognizing the innovative and holistic exhibit planning and design process that took place, the Association of Zoos and Aquariums honored Riverbanks with the Significant Achievement Award for its avian program in 2002.

The Ndoki Forest (pronounced N'doe kee) also opened to the public in 2002 and boasted three and a half acres of new animal exhibits, lush plantings, and upgraded visitor services. The exhibit was named after a remote river in central Africa. Riverbanks set out to re-create this part of the world as a sanctuary for gorillas and elephants.

Riverbanks' habitat horticulture staff planted thousands of trees, shrubs, plants, and grasses after painstakingly researching the environment of the Congo, the area Ndoki Forest was to mimic. They re-created the look with available plants suited for the area. Bamboo, palms, and banana trees take the visitor's imagination on safari when viewing the Ndoki complex. Grassy areas, known as *bais*, completed the realistic look

A young visitor feeds browse to a giraffe. Photograph by Richard W. Rokes.

and offered spots for the gorillas to relax and browse on their daily treats.

Today visitors can watch the gorillas from inside Base Camp as well as from

A young zoo guest enjoys feeding a sociable lorikeet. Photograph by Robin Vondrak Photography.

Popular Family Fun

More than 200 AZA-accredited zoos and aquariums attracted over 175 million visitors in 2011. Approximately 50 million visitors were children, making accredited zoos and aquariums some of the best places for families to connect with nature and each other.

observation points within Ndoki Forest. The gorillas have many places for exploration. To engage the animals, the keepers as well as the horticultural staff make frequent changes to the habitat.

The landscaping for the elephant exhibit encircles the habitat with little planting within the exhibit except for grasses. The focal point is the 12-foot deep, 250,000-gallon watering hole, where visitors can stand on a "dock" to observe the elephants. Daily demonstrations show visitors the training each elephant receives to maintain health and well-being.

Meerkats also enjoy a spacious area created to resemble the arid plains of their home, complete with hollow logs and many places for these curious little animals to explore and dig. These entertaining creatures spend their days cavorting about in search of food and fun. They groom each other, wrestle, play, and show curiosity about their surroundings; however, they never forget to be on alert, with at least one meerkat always on guard duty, standing tall and on the lookout.

The Outback Comes to the Zoo

There is no question that koalas rank among the most adored of all creatures. A survey of animal icons ranked the koala second only to the giant panda in terms of worldwide public recognition. A casual conversation at a cocktail party led directly to Riverbanks acquiring these rare and captivating animals.

In the fall of 1999 the University of South Carolina hosted a reception at Riverbanks

(top) The new Birdhouse at Riverbanks won the AZA Exhibit Award in 2002 for its innovative avian program. Photograph by Matt Croxton. (bottom) A perspective of the gorilla yard that few get to see. The elephants can be seen in the background. Photograph by Lorianne Riggin.

(facing) The lush surroundings of the Ndoki Forest exhibit help mimic the gorilla's natural habitat. Photograph by Richard W. Rokes. (left) Guests were thrilled when the new elephant exhibit opened with African elephants.

An Enormous Job

Providing daily care to Riverbanks' four African elephants is extremely demanding and physically challenging. Six keepers are responsible for carrying out the rigorous duties of elephant care 365 days per year, rain or shine, hot or cold. Each day this dedicated team relocates about 1,200 pounds of manure, scrubs a 5,000-square-foot barn, rakes the entire three-quarter-acre exhibit from top to bottom, and lifts 15 to 20 bales of hay.

Slender-tailed meerkat on the lookout.

and wondered if there was any way Riverbanks could benefit. They were especially interested in knowing if obtaining koalas was a possibility, since most people are fascinated with this species.

Given their highly restrictive diet of eucalyptus, koalas are extremely difficult to maintain in captivity. But, of all things, the California gold rush was a direct contributor to the future success of koalas in captivity. It was during the gold rush that Australian emigrants first introduced the eucalyptus tree to the Pacific Coast state. Before long several species of eucalyptus had become firmly established along the West Coast. These trees paved the way for three California zoos to ultimately establish the largest colonies of koalas outside Australia. These zoos—Los Angeles, San Francisco, and San Diego—have kept koalas off and on throughout much of the past seventy-five years.

Beyond the West Coast zoos, few zoological parks have imported koalas. This is not just a result of their restricted diet but also the reluctance of the Australian federal government to export what is essentially a national treasure.

Not to be deterred, the alliance soon contacted the Queensland government about koalas, setting in motion an incredibly long and complicated chain of events. Nearly

Botanical Garden for students participating in its Masters in International Business program. While at the reception, Zoo Director Satch Krantz engaged in a conversation with staff members from the Central Carolina Economic Development Alliance. The alliance members mentioned that South Carolina had just entered into a sister-state relationship with Queensland, Australia,

STATUS—Uncommon

WHERE IN THE WORLD—At the zoo king penguins can be seen inside the Penguin Coast exhibit in the Birdhouse at Riverbanks. In the wild king penguins live in the outer parts of Antarctica as well as Tierra de Fuego and the Falkland Islands.

ON THE MENU—Penguins dine on fish such as herring, capelin, smelt, and silversides. In the wild small bioluminescent fish called lantern fish make up the bulk of their diet.

CLAIM TO FAME—These beloved birds are survivors. They can withstand the brutal winds and frozen temperatures of the Antarctic.

AMAZING ADAPTATION—Penguins grow up to 70 feathers per square inch for warmth. They also can dive between 300 and 1,000 feet in pursuit of food.

COOL CHARACTERISTICS—The waddling gait of penguins on land belies their supreme swimming ability once in water.

KEEPER'S NOTE—Riverbanks currently has four king penguins; three males and one female. King penguins actually have a very unique form of incubation. They, like the emperor penguin, will incubate a single egg on top of their feet. The big difference between kings and emperors is that the male and female king penguin share the responsibility of incubating the egg. You can see this sharing of responsibility at Riverbanks during king penguin–breeding season, which usually begins in July. They have an almost two-month-long incubation period during which time the incubating pair will pick a spot in the exhibit and stay in this area for the entire incubation, taking turns with the egg every so often.

RIVERBANKS' ROLE—In 2003 members of the zoo staff carried king penguin eggs from the Detroit Zoo back to Riverbanks. The eggs were incubated, and the hatched chicks successfully hand-reared. The young birds grew up in the Penguin Coast exhibit and have remained at the zoo.

King penguins. Riverbanks currently houses four king penguins, thirteen rockhopper penguins, and seven gentoo penguins.

A red-necked wallaby joey pokes out of his mother's pouch. Photograph by Richard W. Rokes.

three years later these efforts would result in koalas arriving at Riverbanks.

Without question this was the most complex animal acquisition in Riverbanks' history. Before completion it required the Queensland government to negotiate a gift of two male koalas from a Japanese zoo in exchange for a small collection of North American animals. And before the first animal arrived in South Carolina, the zoo staff had to arrange for biweekly shipments of eucalyptus from Miami and Phoenix.

Nevertheless two male koalas arrived at Riverbanks in January 2002 from the Hirakawa Zoo in Japan. Slightly more than a year later, two female koalas were transferred to Riverbanks from the David Fleay Wildlife Park on Queensland's Gold Coast. These four koalas were the first to be authorized by the Australian government for transfer to the United States since 1990.

None of this would have been possible without the assistance of Peter Beattie, the premier of Queensland, Australia, and Jim Hodges, South Carolina's governor at the time. Premier Beattie declared the koalas a state gift from the citizens of Queensland to the citizens of South Carolina.

When you visit Koala Knockabout at Riverbanks, chances are you will see the koalas at rest. Koalas feed about four

Koala. Photograph by Richard W. Rokes.

hours a day. The remainder of their time is spent sleeping.

Feats of Animal Dexterity

There is an old adage among zoo directors and curators: any animal is capable of doing anything at any time. The following two stories provide prefect examples of this phenomenon.

All the zoo's dangerous animals are housed behind multiple barriers. So it is possible for an animal to "escape" from one of these barriers yet remain contained within the exhibit or barn and still be separated from human contact. The final barrier, the one separating the animal from the public or employees, is known as the primary barrier, or primary containment.

Koala—*Phascolarctos cinereus*

STATUS—Lower risk, near threatened.

WHERE IN THE WORLD—Koalas are native to Australia. At Riverbanks these popular mammals reside in the Koala Knockabout exhibit.

ON THE MENU—The koala is one of the zoo's pickiest eaters, feeding exclusively on eucalyptus. Depending on their individual needs, the koalas are offered between 10 to 20 pounds of eucalyptus per day. Because of their slow metabolism, however, they consume only a fraction of what is offered and forage only on the fresh, succulent growth. Keepers closely monitor the koalas' food consumption as part of the daily routine.

COOL CHARACTERISTICS—Koalas are particularly inactive, spending between 18 and 20 hours a day resting and

Koala and joey. Photograph by Ron Brasington.

sleeping. The best time to see a koala awake is at mealtime.

KEEPER'S NOTE—Koalas are marsupials. The female has a pouch for her young, known as a "joey." When a joey is born, it is the size of a jelly bean and weighs less than a penny. The miniature marsupial stays in its mother's pouch for about six months while it continues to develop. When ready to explore, it emerges from the pouch very slowly. First it will stick out a hand, and then a foot and maybe an ear. Once it makes its way out of the pouch completely, the joey will cling to its mother's back as it learns to eat eucalyptus leaves and climb branches. The joey will remain dependent on its mom for 12 months.

Like every zoo, Riverbanks has experienced its share of escapes. The vast majority of escapes involve small or nondangerous animals and usually occur when an animal is being transferred from one area of the zoo to another, such as from its exhibit to the hospital. But, in spite of all the safeguards, dangerous animals have escaped their primary containment on two separate occasions over the past thirty-eight years. Each escape resulted from a feat of animal dexterity.

A few months after the zoo opened in 1974, a female polar bear escaped from her exhibit and roamed the grounds for about twenty minutes. The bear had jumped down into the fourteen-foot-deep moat that separates the exhibit from the public the day before and was unable to climb back onto the exhibit. There was a flaw in the exhibit's design, and this had become a regular occurrence, so the zoo's maintenance department constructed a wooden ramp to help facilitate a safe and quick exit for the bears. The ramp was smooth on one side but contained a series of wooden cleats on the other side that allowed the bear to gain a foothold. When necessary, the ramp would be lowered into the moat from the public sidewalk, and then pushed back toward the exhibit side of the moat, allowing the bears to safely climb out.

(top) While thousands of animals have been born and hatched at Riverbanks over the past forty years, perhaps none has been as adorable as these baby polar bears. Even though the zoo's polar bears have been gone since 2001, guests still ask for them; Riverbanks joined a number of zoos throughout the southern tier of the United States in sending their polar bears to cooler climes. (bottom) The zoo has prided itself on innovative displays such as the polar bear exhibit with an underwater viewing area, seen here under construction.

RIVERBANKS ZOO AND GARDEN

Wild about Riverbanks

Any longtime Riverbanks Zoo member may recall some of the many individual animals that have resided at the zoo over the years, such as Olga the elephant, Montgomery the hippo, Garfield the great horned owl, Blondie the horse, and Baines the Hamadryas baboon. These charming animals made wonderful memories for all of the zoo's visitors, but for me, they inspired a career and lifelong obsession. Back in those days the summer camp program was called WildWeeks, and I attended every single year. Once I was too old for the zoo camp programs I volunteered in the zoo's animal hospital. Cleaning up after quarantine animals, scrubbing stalls and changing newspaper in the injured owl cages in our raptor rehabilitation center don't sound like typical weekend activities for a high school student, but I looked forward to it all week long. Naturally I studied wildlife biology in college, did an internship with exotic cats and applied to Riverbanks to be a zookeeper after graduation. But this is no Cinderella story, I was declined. In fact, I applied to Riverbanks three times and even volunteered briefly before finally being offered a part-time position. After working [at the zoo] for 9 months I was offered the Swing Keeper position in the mammal department in 2009. This position allows me to work with all of the fascinating species in [the zoo's] mammal collection. My passion had finally turned into a career at a facility that constantly challenges me, encourages me to grow, and feels like home.

Stacy Hitt, Riverbanks Mammal Keeper

Only this time the bear balked. In spite of multiple attempts to get her to use the ramp, the bear stayed defiantly in the bottom of the moat. At the end of the day, the frustrated keepers pulled the heavy ramp back to the vertical public side of the moat, tied it to the steel handrail and went home. The bear and ramp remained in the moat all night, until 9:45 the following morning. Then the bear managed to spin the ramp 180 degrees, thus gaining access to the wooden cleats. She then managed to climb fourteen feet straight up to the top of the moat wall and out onto the public sidewalk.

(left) During the internal follow-up investigation to the 2009 gorilla incident, Curator of Mammals John Davis demonstrated the strength of a single piece of bamboo that gave a gorilla the impetus to break out of his containment. Photograph by Sue Pfaff. (right) A muddy footprint on the exhibit wall near the site of the broken bamboo provided further evidence of the gorilla's escape route. Photograph by Sue Pfaff.

By this time nearly fifty employees and a number of construction workers were spread throughout the zoo grounds. Fortunately the zoo opened to the public at 10:00 A.M. during its first few years of operation, so there were no guests on site—at least not when she climbed out!

The bear lumbered along the sidewalk to the sea lion exhibit, where she leaned over the pool wall and swatted at the sea lions as they swam by. She then traveled to what is now the Conservation Outpost (also known as the Small Mammal Tunnel), at the time still under construction. Several terrified

A gorilla on the move in the Ndoki Forest exhibit. Photograph by Ron Brasington.

construction workers saw the approaching bear and quickly climbed to the roof of the building, pulling the ladders up after them. Like most escaped animals, she eventually headed back toward her exhibit, but only after detouring to the elephant barn, where she stuck her head inside the door to take a peek at the three screaming pachyderms.

By this time word of the escape had reached the administration building. Armed with tranquilizer guns, two members of the staff, including future zoo director Satch Krantz, ran to the polar bear exhibit. The bear was safely darted as she paced back and forth along the top of her exhibit moat. It would be thirty-five more years before another dangerous animal would escape.

On June 12, 2009, at 9:23 A.M., one of the zoo's three male gorillas climbed out of his enclosure, using a single piece of low-hanging rain-soaked bamboo. For the next four minutes he roamed up and down the sidewalk in front of the one-acre exhibit, beating his chest and running past several members of the public and two concession-stand employees. One of the employees was injured when the gorilla knocked his feet out from under him and pushed on his legs and arms. The 400-pound gorilla then jumped back into the exhibit.

Approximately three hundred guests were in the park at the time of the incident, all of whom were escorted to safe and secure locations. Forty-five minutes after the escape, the park reopened and was fully operational. Ironically, and perhaps a sign of the times, numerous cell-phone calls were made from zoo visitors to the local media during this period, but none of the guests called 911.

During the thirty-five years separating these two escapes, the Association of Zoos and Aquariums adopted a mandatory accreditation program. As part of the accreditation program, member zoos are required not only to have a dangerous animal escape plan but also to conduct annual drills. By the time the gorilla escaped from

(top) Before 2002 the zoo's elephants were trained to perform tricks. (bottom) Up until the time when Riverbanks' elephants were transferred to other zoos, prior to the Zoo 2002 expansion, they were often taken to the banks of the Saluda River where they were allowed to roam before the zoo opened in the morning.

Raspberry Rose Mallow—*Hibiscus* 'Raspberry Rose'

COLOR: Deep pink-rose
BLOOMING PERIOD: Summer
TYPE: Flowering perennial
SIZE: 6 to 7 feet tall by 8 to 10 feet wide
EXPOSURE: Full Sun

This fabulous plant produces 10-inch diameter rose-pink flowers all summer long. Great for making a dramatic impact in the garden. Look no further than 'Raspberry Rose' when you want a tropical look in your garden.

The outstretched petals really stand out. Photograph by Andy Cabe.

its habitat in 2009, Riverbanks' senior animal staff had conducted these drills and reacted quickly and effectively, almost by instinct.

A Day in the Life of the Zoo

Some say that zoos are like small towns. The "town" of Riverbanks has approximately two thousand residents, a hospital, a school, shops and restaurants, public safety officers, and a public works department. Most zoo managers will tell you that no two days are ever the same. While this is certainly true, there is a rhythm to each twenty-four-hour period. The following depicts a typical day at Riverbanks.

7:00 A.M.

The workday begins with the grounds and custodial departments cleaning the zoo and garden's vast public spaces. Nearly two miles of sidewalks are blown clean and more than 100 trash cans are emptied prior to the 9:00 A.M. opening. By day's end cleaning crews scour 200,000 square-feet of indoor public spaces.

Members of the horticulture staff (both zoo and garden) dig into their work before the first guests arrive. This is the best time to escape the heat of summer and perform tasks in and around public spaces. On this day the garden staff will plant 3,000 spring bulbs. Each year, Riverbanks Botanical Garden plants 11,970 pansies, 22,015 bulbs and 11,683 winter veggies.

Riverbanks' maintenance technicians also arrive. For these employees each day is unique. The maintenance needs of the zoo and garden are as varied as they are extensive. While the day begins with a list of preventive maintenance projects, the techs prepare themselves for unexpected problems such as clogged drains, stuck doors, flat tires, and broken air conditioners.

8:00 A.M.

The animal care staff reports for duty. Since the zoo opens at 9:00 A.M., keepers quickly disperse among the various buildings and exhibits to turn on lights and carefully scrutinize and count each of the two thousand animals. Food pans are inspected to ensure animal diets have been consumed overnight, and the staff even examine the animals' feces. A keeper immediately notices that a male tiger's stool appears abnormal and notifies the hospital staff by radio. All observations are noted on a daily report form,

By the Numbers

Each year, Riverbanks Zoo and Garden welcomes more than 1 million guests. That's an average of 2,754 people each day—the size of the town of Folly Beach. Every year our visitors eat more than 3 tons of hot dogs, consume 191,000 gallons of soft drinks, use 941 miles of toilet paper, and fill more than 60,000 trash bags.

Riverbanks is blessed with wonderfully talented and dedicated employees. Here two maintenance technicians work on the old Boomerang Gift Shop.

Mammal keeper Windsor Cowart feeds the lemurs. Photograph by Richard W. Rokes.

which is later reviewed by members of the animal management team.

8:15 A.M.

Exhibit prep begins. Keepers collect food and droppings from the day before as well as prepare environmental enrichment items, such as sunflower seeds or raisins, for most animals. While scattering peanuts in the gorilla exhibit, a keeper notices one of the gorillas has pulled a large shrub out of the ground by its roots and notifies the horticulture team for advice and assistance.

8:30 A.M.

The guest services team—the largest contingent of Riverbanks employees—begins their day. Seventy-five staff members fan out across the zoo and garden to sell tickets, operate the carousel, bake pizzas, and pour ICEEs for today's three thousand expected guests. The administrative staff—finance, membership, marketing, and human resources—also arrives.

9:00 A.M.

Keepers open appropriate doors to provide the animals with access to their outdoor exhibits. The pace picks up as the first visitors enter the park and the first tram of the day makes its way from the Botanical Garden. A guest stops by the Elephant's Trunk

Gift Shop; she needs a bandage for her three-year-old's finger.

9:15 A.M.

At the zoo's front entrance, a motor coach with fifty middle-school students and chaperones from Newberry breaks down. Riverbanks' public safety team responds to the major traffic jam developing in the parking lot.

9:30 A.M.

A guest encounters a black rat snake along a path in the Botanical Garden. Members of the staff are dispatched to catch the snake and release it along the river.

10:00 A.M.

Kenya Café as well as several other food stands and carts around the zoo open for business.

10:15 A.M.

Public safety helps locate a lost child— or is it the parent who was lost?

10:30 A.M.

A frantic call comes in from an emergency room physician in Charlotte, North Carolina. The facility has just admitted a local resident who was bitten by his pet cobra, and the staff are desperate for cobra

Bird keeper Lisa Galloway feeds a hornbill. Photograph by Richard W. Rokes.

What's All the Stink About?

Riverbanks comPOOst, recipient of the 2012 Earth Day Award by South Carolina Department of Health and Environmental Control, is 100 percent all-natural composted Zoo poo—comPOOst is produced by some of Riverbanks Zoo's most famous animals: elephants, giraffes, and zebras.

Riverbanks comPOOst logo designed by the artists at Chernoff Newman.

(top) Since 2006 Riverbanks' trams have transported more than 1.8 million visitors between the zoo and garden, logging more than seventy thousand miles inside the park. (bottom) A dedicated volunteer engages guests at the daily dive demonstration. In 2011 the zoo's education volunteers gave more than 1,050 hours of their time to inspire conservation action in 119,000 visitors.

antivenom. The zoo's supply of antivenom is transported to Palmetto Richland Hospital and then flown by helicopter to Charlotte. This means that for the next three months the zoo's reptile keepers are at risk should they be bitten. Riverbanks' curator of herpetology makes a call to his counterpart at Zoo Atlanta and notifies him that his zoo will be our back-up supplier until the antivenom is replaced.

11:00 A.M.

A tractor-trailer load of alfalfa hay arrives and is parked behind the elephant barn.

11:15 A.M.

An excited young man approaches a public safety officer. He and several friends were rafting down the Saluda River and overturned in the rapids. One of his friends is missing. A 911 call goes out, and for the next several hours the west end of the parking lot is ablaze with flashing red and blue lights as several agencies respond.

11:30 A.M.

One of the bird keepers calls the hospital. A Toco toucan does not look well, and she would like for someone to look at it.

11:45 A.M.

The zoo's switchboard operator receives a call from two men arguing over which is stronger, a gorilla or an orangutan, and they have bet a six-pack of beer on the outcome. She routes the call to the curator of mammals. Later in the day the operator will route a call to the curator of birds to answer a bird-related crossword-puzzle query.

11:50 A.M.

A guest approaches the front-gate attendant. He is leaving the zoo and discovers that his car battery is dead. Public safety is dispatched with jumper cables.

Noon

Most departments begin their lunch hour; however, several members of the maintenance department are in the middle of repairing the penguin chiller and cannot stop. The work continues until mid-afternoon, when they are finally able to grab a bite to eat. A group of one hundred employees from a local insurance company has rented the Magnolia Room in the Botanical Garden Visitor's Center for a training seminar. They break for lunch and are transported by tram to the zoo for a barbeque picnic in Safari Camp.

Did You Know?

Riverbanks Zoo's Adventure Tours give visitors a behind-the-scenes look at the challenges of animal care and the amazing efforts that go into creating and sustaining a world-class zoo.

Adventure Tours offer various opportunities for guests to get up-close with the animals. Children are seen here behind the scenes with a leaf-tailed gecko. Photograph by Robin Vondrak Photography.

Riverbanks has been blessed with many talented employees. Step Taylor, 2002 Employee of the Year, cradles a young Nubian goat.

1:30 P.M.

Riverbanks' veterinarian begins to immobilize and examine a young giraffe that has been limping for several days. Six other employees will also be involved. This procedure will take almost three hours, not including the time involved in planning. A keeper will remain with the animal throughout the night as it recovers from the anesthesia.

1:45 P.M.

While planting bulbs a garden volunteer accidentally cuts an irrigation line, sending a geyser of water fifteen feet into the air. Water from the Saluda River is not only used to irrigate zoo and garden plants, it is also used to clean most of the zoo's large barns and to fill various pools. Because of the broken irrigation line, the system is temporarily shut down, and for the next two hours the zoo must rely on the City of Columbia for its water, costing several hundreds of dollars in the interim.

2:00 P.M.

A meeting takes place in the Discovery Center library. The zoo has been notified that a portion of the railroad crossing at the entrance to the parking lot will be replaced the following week. The staff needs to plan how vehicles will be routed safely around the construction site. The zoo's chief operating officer, director of facilities management, and director of guest services attend, along with representatives of the railroad.

Riverbanks maintains dozens of different species of venomous snakes. Many of these are exotic species and include some of the most dangerous animals on the planet, including mambas, king cobras, bushmasters, and giant rattlesnakes. The ability to work safely with venomous snakes is quite simple, especially if certain basic safety rules are followed. Riverbanks has strict policies that dictate how staff will interact with venomous snakes, and because of that along with a good measure of common sense, the zoo has never had a venomous snakebite.

To prepare for the remote possibility that a staff member is envenomated, Riverbanks maintains a stock of antivenoms for use in the medical treatment of a snakebite. Virtually all of the antivenoms at the zoo are of foreign manufacture and are not FDA approved drugs. In order to be able to import and stock these antivenoms, Riverbanks had to first acquire an investigational new drug permit and then obtain a permit before each importation.

The zoo typically keeps ten different antivenoms on hand. Some are effective against the venoms of many species; others are effective against only one. Antivenoms are produced to supply coverage for the world's most dangerous snakes—species that have a potent venom and are also responsible for a significant number of envenomations.

Although Riverbanks has never had to use antivenom for its staff, several times each year the zoo has provided antivenom for the medical treatment of soldiers and private hobbyists who were bitten by exotic venomous snakes.

Cottonmouth. Photograph by Richard W. Rokes.

2:30 P.M.

The missing young man from the earlier river raft spill is found clinging to a boulder in the river. He is safely rescued.

3:00 P.M.

A visitor is stung by a bee and receives first aid from a member of the public safety staff.

3:15 P.M.

The garden takes a call from a homeowner who wants to know the best place in Columbia to buy daylilies.

3:30 P.M.

A five-year-old child approaches a public safety officer and says that he cannot find his classmates. A quick review of the daily admission record indicates that the group (a daycare center from Florence, South Carolina) left the park thirty minutes ago. The daycare is called and confirms that the child is registered there and was on a field trip to Riverbanks. A member of the public services department calls the child's parents as well as the police. Since the parents must drive from Florence, a staff member remains with the child until they arrive. A number of reports are filled out by everyone involved in the incident, including law enforcement and the Department of Social Services.

4:30 P.M.

The attendant at the information kiosk meets a family from Ohio. They stopped by Riverbanks on their way to Disney World, expecting to stay a couple of hours. Instead they have been in the zoo for nearly five hours and have decided to spend the night in Columbia. They ask for hotel and restaurant recommendations.

4:45 P.M.

Two bird keepers leave for the airport to pick up a penguin that has been flown to Columbia from the St. Louis Zoo.

5:00 P.M.

Most employees head home. A public safety officer will remain on duty throughout the night; a keeper will sleep in the barn with the young giraffe; another keeper will return later in the evening to feed a baby macaw.

While some of these occurrences may seem unusual, they actually do occur at Riverbanks with some frequency, such as a child left behind on a school outing. Notably few of these incidents are animal-related. This is typical of most zoos: people-related incidents far exceed those caused by animals.

Signature Events at Riverbanks

Cultural attractions such as zoos, museums, and public gardens often conduct special events to generate publicity and raise money. Riverbanks is no exception. The zoo first began hosting special events in the early 1980s and continues to do so today. Some events are held one day a year while others take place over a number of days and nights. Together these events have grown so large and complex that a dedicated events department was established in 2004.

WINE TASTING AT RIVERBANKS BOTANICAL GARDEN

Time of year: One night in April.

Started: 2004.

General format: After-hours wine tasting, live jazz, light bites.

Annual attendance: 800.

What it takes: 80 volunteers, 20 staff, 744 bottles of wine.

Of note: The first Wine Tasting event was managed in part by Clear Channel; Riverbanks began orchestrating the event in 2005.

BREW AT THE ZOO

Time of year: First Friday in August.

Started: 2006.

General format: Night in the zoo for grown-ups with beer sampling, live music, and animal presentations.

Annual attendance: 1,800.

(top) Guests savoring the sights, scents, and sounds of the wine tasting at Riverbanks Botanical Garden. Photograph by Robin Vondrak Photography. (bottom) Souvenir glasses from Brew at the Zoo, 2008. Photograph by Robin Vondrak Photography.

(top) An old jeep was transformed into a fruit and cheese display at the 2006 Wild Things Safari. (bottom) When it comes to daily attendance, Boo at the Zoo outshines the Lights before Christmas. On average the popular Halloween Spooktacular draws 2,500 guests per night as opposed to the 1,750 nightly visitors who attend Lights before Christmas. Photograph by Matt Croxton.

What it takes: 30 staff, 130 volunteers, 110 specialty, import, and domestic brews; more than 20,000 samples poured.

Of note: Initially held on the first Saturday in August, the event was moved to Friday in 2012 to increase participation and improve logistics.

RIVERBANKS ZOOFARI

Time of year: One night in September or October.

Started: 1999. Originally dubbed Wild Things Safari, the fundraiser's name was changed in 2006.

General format: Epicurean "safari" through the zoo; entertainment; silent and live auctions.

Annual attendance: 400–800.

What it takes: 30 staff, 40 volunteers, 12 live auction items, 50 silent auction items.

Of note: The first "zoofaris" offered by Riverbanks were group trips to the North Carolina Zoo in the early 1980s.

BOO AT THE ZOO

Time of year: 12 to 13 nights in October.

Started: 2003.

General format: Safe family-friendly trick-or-treating "Spooktacular" on the nights leading up to Halloween.

Annual attendance: 30,000 plus.

Wild about Riverbanks

To the Wonderful People at the Columbia SC Zoo,

I am so happy to get to share one of the happiest days of my life with ya'll. When my children were little the three of us and their grandmother would go to the zoo every chance we could get. It's like a second home for us. [Our] most favorite times would be when it was opened at night. We would get a motel room so that we could go to the zoo during the day and would leave when the zoo closed. We would rest at the motel, then go back to the zoo, for the night event. Christmas time is wonderful but Halloween is the best. It is so safe for the kids to dress up and go trick or treating at the zoo. We would also have hot chocolate and make smores.

Well now I'm a grandmother and so happy that in Oct 2011 four generations went to the zoo. My mother, daughter, grandbaby, and I had a blast. We went back that night to go trick or treating, but this time ya'll had a wonderful DJ. He had a special talent and with everybody that came in to the zoo he connected with them. You just had to get up and dance with him. Adults, children, the young and the old would follow him dancing we almost forgot to go trick or treating, but we did it and it was wonderful. The grandbaby loved it. We also had hot chocolate and made smores again. It was a wonderful way to end the night. Thank ya'll for giving me this special gift that I will treasure forever.

Deann Neely Quick, Hephzibah, GA

What it takes: 50 staff, 1,000 volunteers, 7,800 pounds of candy, 850 gallons of Frankenstein's Foam Zone suds.

Of note: The first Halloween Spooktacular at Riverbanks kicked off in October 1989. As a result of various logistical challenges, the initial series was discontinued a few years later. The event was eventually revitalized as today's very popular Boo at the Zoo.

Lights Before Christmas

Time of year: Forty nights through November and December.

Started: 1987.

Format: nightly showcase of holiday lights throughout the zoo; "snows" nightly.

Annual attendance: 70,000 guests.

What it takes: 30 staff, 100 volunteers, 80 elves, 400 animated images, 600 gallons of artificial snow, 500,000 strands of lights.

Of note: Preparations for Lights Before Christmas begin as early as July. Trees are unwrapped immediately after the event ends to allow for growth before re-wrapping for next season.

(facing) Three orphaned grizzly bear cubs were rescued in Alaska in early 2002. Two of the brothers, Butch and Sundance, arrived at Riverbanks in September that year and since then have become some of the best-liked residents at the zoo. Photograph by Ron Brasington.

Of the hundreds of sparkling trees and images showcased during Lights Before Christmas, these two magnificent trees really shine.

Chapter 6

INTO THE FUTURE

A Powerful Economic Engine

In 2008 the University of South Carolina's College of Hospitality, Retail, and Sport Management conducted a comprehensive study to determine the annual financial contributions of Riverbanks Zoo and Garden on the economy of Richland and Lexington Counties. The report illustrated the economic impact of both tourism and operational spending associated with Riverbanks and proved that the zoo and garden is a powerful economic driver within the local economy.

Measuring only the financial contribution of Riverbanks, this study did not include assessments of social benefits, such as the educational and cultural enrichment of children and families within the community. Nor did it include other less measurable economic benefits such as decisions by businesses to locate in Richland and Lexington Counties because of Riverbanks or an increase in market value of properties located near Riverbanks.

Most notably the study revealed that Riverbanks generated $60.8 million in

(facing) Sea lions were always a crowd favorite at Riverbanks, but their exhibit deteriorated and was demolished in the summer of 2009. With the recent bond issue, Riverbanks looks forward to bringing back the popular pinnepeds in a bigger and better exhibit with underwater viewing. Photograph by Richard W. Rokes.

A crowd of visitors waiting to board the tram to the Botanical Garden.

local business sales, $42.8 million of which was generated as a result of travel-related expenses associated with tourists who visited Riverbanks and $18 million as a result of Riverbanks operations. The report found that not only does Riverbanks have a positive impact on local business sales, but it also has a significant impact on job creation in the Midlands. The study indicated that Riverbanks generated 723 jobs in the community, resulting in $18.3 million in employee compensation at local businesses.

Making Tracks

It's highly improbable that when a group of Columbia business leaders came together in the early 1960s to plan a modest zoo for Columbia's children they believed it would

become South Carolina's largest attraction and the most attended zoo in the southeastern United States. Likewise, when the zoo opened in April 1974, hardly anyone envisioned it becoming one of America's most successful zoological parks and botanical gardens. So, what does the future hold in store as Riverbanks approaches its fifth decade of existence?

In many ways the future of Riverbanks Zoo and Garden may be more difficult to predict than at any time in its past. There is no doubt that zoos are rapidly changing— mostly for the better. With today's increased knowledge of animal behavior and veterinary medicine, Riverbanks is able to provide the animals with optimal care, helping to ensure their physical and psychological well-being. Vast improvements in exhibit design mean that the animals are living in environments that better simulate the wild and stimulate natural behaviors. But modern zoos are also changing in other, perhaps less desirable ways.

In the 1970s national and international laws were enacted that severely limited the importation of animals from the wild. The AZA supported these regulations, which were largely intended to stop the trafficking in wildlife (both living and not) for commercial activities such as the exotic pet trade. But the new laws and regulations did

Gloriosa Lily—*Gloriosa superba* 'Rothschildiana'

COLOR: Red and yellow
BLOOMING PERIOD: Summer
TYPE: Tuberous climbing lily
SIZE: 5 to 6 feet tall
EXPOSURE: Full sun

As summer temperatures heat up, the gloriosa lily begins to flower freely. The flower itself is one of the most exquisite beauties of the plant world. The red and yellow recurved petals make this vine

A spectacular lily. Photograph by Andy Cabe.

look like it is engulfed with flames. It needs something to climb on (such as a trellis), or it can be planted at the base of a shrub. Something so pretty shouldn't be this easy to grow!

not discriminate, and it is ironic that zoos suddenly found themselves scrambling for animals. Now some forty years later the variety of wildlife found in AZA institutions has greatly diminished. The phrase "homogenization of zoo collections" was recently coined to describe what could happen in the future, that regardless of which zoo a guest might visit, he will encounter the same animals over and over again.

To help prevent this from occurring, AZA-accredited zoos and aquariums have implemented a number of aggressive breeding programs aimed at ensuring sustainable captive populations. Many of these programs have succeeded, while others have met with limited success. Only time will tell what impact these programs will have on the future of zoos and aquariums. But this is not just a problem facing zoos. As nature becomes more and more fragmented,

These five lion cubs were born at Riverbanks in the summer of 2008. Zoo guests delighted in watching the feisty little felines grow up. They were ultimately transferred to other zoos based on SSP recommendations. Photograph by Ron Brasington.

zoo collections could indeed soon serve as modern-day arks.

Today most cultural attractions are also challenged with declining government funding. This factor has forced Riverbanks to become far more entrepreneurial in its daily operations, and as a result the zoo now offers guests a far better product. The Riverbanks Park Commission and staff are often confronted with issues that appear to contradict the zoo's mission: for instance, how a ropes course or children's train ride could possibly foster an appreciation of living things. Fortunately the staff continues to find ways to connect guests to nature and wildlife, albeit somewhat indirectly, through the mimicking of animal behaviors (such as climbing) or by virtue of location (such as a natural wooded area). In fact hands-on, interactive activities and attractions have proven to enhance the visitor experience, while providing much-needed additional income to help fulfill the zoo's mission.

In this fast-paced, ever-changing society, Americans are living more culturally diverse and technologically demanding lives. Like all zoos Riverbanks will need to evolve to keep up with these changes while at the same time maintaining the intimate setting that has for years appealed to so many. As a result of the changing demands and complexities of running a zoo with more than 1 million visitors a year, in September 2011 Riverbanks Zoo and Garden hired Tommy Stringfellow as its first-ever chief operating officer. Stringfellow was charged with overseeing marketing, guest services, human resources, facilities, and IT.

With no major exhibits to boast since 2002, the Riverbanks Park Commission and staff grew concerned that attendance could suffer without something new to offer visitors. While paid attractions such as the kids train ride and rock wall were value-added experiences, it would only be a matter of time before guests would be looking for

(top) Campers test their climbing skills on the zoo's twenty-six-foot rock wall. (bottom) The Spots 'n' Stripes railroad was a welcome addition for young visitors in 2008. The kids' train travels through a naturally wooded area, helping to maintain a connection with nature.

Red kangaroo. Photograph by Richard W. Rokes.

new animals. The commission began discussions with Richland and Lexington Counties in the fall of 2008 in hopes of seeking a new $40 million bond issue for another major expansion, this time dubbed "Destination Riverbanks." But by January the economy had fallen into a deep recession, and the commission quickly pulled in the reins to wait out the slump. Years passed, and the commission waited.

The Road Ahead

While the possibility of another major expansion slowed because of the economy, the zoo added several new exhibits and animals in an effort to continue to attract new and repeat visitors. Kangaroo Walkabout opened in spring 2010, utilizing the footprint of the demolished sea lion exhibit. The innovative habitat, featuring red kangaroos and red-necked wallabies, provides guests with the opportunity to walk—or hop—along a path that goes directly through the exhibit.

Later in the year the zoo began adding several Indonesian animals. In December 2010 the zoo acquired a babirusa, an exotic tusked pig. Staff retrofitted the old warthog exhibit to create a home for the "deer-pig." A female companion was acquired about two years later, per AZA breeding recommendations.

By the spring of 2012 the Aquarium-Reptile Complex added two juvenile Komodo dragons. The legendary lizards created quite a buzz among guests. And in November 2012 staff redesigned the old hippo exhibit to house a Malayan tapir. The 650-pound mammal generated additional excitement among visitors and staff. Despite a lack of major exhibits since 2002, curiosity about these rare and unusual animals has helped Riverbanks maintain its million-visitor-a-year attendance.

In 2012 the commission decided it was time to make a move with a reduced plan. By the fall of 2012, Richland and Lexington County Councils unanimously approved the single largest bond issue in Riverbanks' history, $32 million. With this generous community backing, Riverbanks will be able to construct a state-of-the art sea lion exhibit (replacing the original that was demolished in 2009); develop a new and improved entrance to accommodate the many visitors to the zoo; build a children's garden on a beautiful two-acre site near the walled garden in the Botanical Garden; expand the parking area; and improve guest amenities and services throughout the zoo and garden. Many of these exciting new additions will come to fruition just in time for the zoo's fortieth anniversary celebration.

(top) Malayan tapir. Photograph by Richard W. Rokes. (bottom) Babirusa. Photograph by Larry Cameron.

Komodo dragons. Photograph by Richard W. Rokes. (facing, top and bottom left) Photographs by Robin Vondrak Photography.

Many challenges await us as we pave our way to a new future, but Riverbanks is up to the challenge. Indeed the Riverbanks Park Commission and the Riverbanks staff love a good challenge and look forward to traveling the road ahead. After all, each day that we can ignite a spark in children's hearts and minds to love a penguin, lion, or tortoise, the more likely they will be later to take action later on in life to protect the zoo's inhabitants. This can help ensure that the plants and animals so appreciated by these children will be around one day for their own children to see. Then we will be another step closer to creating a better future for our children, the animals, and our community.

INDEX

(facing) A sea lion on the rocks. Photograph by Ron Brasington.

About the authors

PALMER "SATCH" KRANTZ began his career
at Riverbanks in Columbia, South Carolina,
in 1974 and has served as its executive director
since 1976, making him one of the longest-
serving zoo directors in the United States. During his career Krantz has twice served as president of the Association of Zoos and Aquariums
and president of the World Association of Zoos
and Aquariums. Most notably Krantz is one
of only three American zoo directors who have
served as president of both organizations. Recipient of the Woodrow Wilson Award for Regional
Cooperation from the Greater Columbia Chamber of Commerce, the International Ambassador
of the Year Award from the Committee of 100,
and the Global Vision Award from the World
Affairs Council, Krantz was most recently recognized as one of the fifty most influential leaders
in Columbia.

MONIQUE BLANCHETTE JACOBS joined the
Riverbanks team in 2001 and currently serves
as manager of Riverbanks Society, communications manager for Riverbanks Zoo and Garden,
and editor of *Riverbanks* magazine. Previously
Jacobs served in membership marketing at a
national nonprofit association and co-owned
a coffee house in Boone, North Carolina.